The Watchdog Concept

THE
WATCHDOG
CONCEPT

*The Press and the Courts
in Nineteenth-Century America*

TIMOTHY W. GLEASON

Iowa State University Press / Ames

For my brothers: Kip, Kevin, and Sean

Timothy W. Gleason is assistant professor in the School of Journalism at the University of Oregon, Eugene, Oregon.

y

First edition, 1990

Library of Congress Cataloging-in-Publication Data

Gleason, Timothy W.
    The watchdog concept : The press and the courts in nineteenth-century America / Timothy W. Gleason. — 1st ed.
        p.   cm.
    Bibliography: p.
    Includes index.
    ISBN 0-8138-0152-4
    1. Freedom of the press—United States—History. 2. Press and politics—United States—History. I. Title.
KF4774.G57 1990
342.73′0853—dc20
[347.302853]   89–15265

CONTENTS

Preface
vii

PREFACE

—————————————

Y search for the origins of the watchdog concept of freedom of the press began with a question about the failure of the concept in mass media litigation. Why have courts not accepted claims based on the press's self-defined role as the public's watchdog? In attempting to answer the question, this study became a search for the origins of the watchdog and an examination of the nature of the concept of freedom of the press.

The tradition, some would argue the myth, of the press as a public watchdog is a glorious one, rich with crusading editors and enterprising reporters ferreting out corruption and malfeasance. Within the journalism community that tradition fuels the journalistic fire that burns in many if not all of the best in the business. Journalists frequently describe themselves as "representatives of the public," or as the "eyes and ears of the public" and assert a right to speak and publish based not on their right as citizens but on their role as the public's servant. This same concept of the press is found in legal arguments in free-press case law.

But, as Professor William Van Alstyne and others have shown, the watchdog tradition of the press is in conflict with the dominant liberal concept of freedom of the press found in twentieth-century First Amendment law. That concept of freedom of the press is based on the individual's right to "think as you will and speak as you think," while the watchdog concept places the press in a subservient relation to the public.

The conflict between the individual-rights concept of freedom of the press and the watchdog concept provides a means of distinguishing the two concepts and suggests a way of explaining the failure of the watchdog. But if the watchdog concept is not in agreement with First Amendment theory, then where and how did it emerge in free-press law?

Traditionally, the history of freedom of the press in the United States has been seen as an evolution of steadily expanding liberty. The focus of free-press history has been legal doctrine as defined by the original intent of the framers and the opinions of the Supreme Court of the United States beginning with *Schenk v. United States* in 1919. However, the work of the *Legal Realists*, the *Law and Society* movement, and now the *Critical Legal Studies* movement shows that the study of legal history cannot be confined to the study of doctrinal change in a vacuum.

The history of free-press law is a history of litigation. The development of the watchdog concept did not take place in the quiet, thoughtful environment of theorists and philosophers, but in the heat of courtroom battles over the legal protections given to newspapers. Thus, the practice of free-press law and the nature of legal practice became a focus of this research. Given the emphasis in First Amendment history on original intent and twentieth-century Supreme Court opinions, the black letter legal practice of free-press law in the nineteenth century raises significant questions about the importance of the jurisprudence of original intent in the development of First Amendment doctrine.

A libertarian view of the original intent of the framers has been the point of departure for the twentieth-century discussion of freedom of the press in the United States. Zechariah Chafee established the framework in *Freedom of Speech*, published in 1920, and Leonard Levy redefined it in *Legacy of Suppression*, published in 1960. Following Levy's revisionist view of the meaning of the press clause in 1791, a group of scholars attempted to refute Levy. That discourse influenced this book.

Levy suggests that law and theory are central to understanding the framers' concept of freedom of the press. He did not find fully developed libertarian theories of freedom of the press, but he did find clear government authority to punish criticism of government. Based on this evidence, Levy asserts, "the press cannot be free—or not as free as it should be."

Dwight Teeter and others argue that Levy "overvalue[d] courts and law and theory at the expense of journalistic practice." Jeffery A. Smith, in *Printers and Press Freedom*, the most extensive response to Levy, argues that the practice of journalism in the colonial and revolutionary period, when examined in the context of radical Whig and enlightenment thought, shows that a "general libertarian press ideology" existed in 1791. This practice and ideology, Smith claims, defines the meaning of freedom of the press in the First Amendment.

While Levy and his critics seem to disagree about the meaning of freedom of the press, in fact they are looking at different questions. Levy treats freedom of the press, rightly I think, as an individual right to be defined in terms of legal constraints on government's power to censor or punish expression. The fact that government cannot or does not exercise its power is not evidence of a different concept of the legal right. Smith views the practice of freedom of the press through the prism of enlightenment thought and radical Whig ideology and finds a more libertarian concept of freedom of the press that he extends to the legal right.

Norman Rosenberg, in *Protecting the Best Men*, a groundbreaking work on the history of libel law, warns that "the writing of First Amendment history contains numerous pitfalls . . . words such as 'freedom' and 'libertarian' . . . must be grounded in an historical setting." As the discourse generated by Levy's work shows, a clear understanding of the nature of the concept of freedom of the press is essential to productive pursuit of the meaning of freedom of the press.

This book shows that while journalistic practice and free-press theory are important to our understanding of the development of free-press law, they are not the central influences on the shaping of that law. At least in the nineteenth century, pragmatic black letter law and the demands of litigation shaped the law of freedom of the press, including the watchdog concept.

Professor Don R. Pember, Director of the School of Communications, University of Washington, and Professor Richard F. Carter, School of Communications, University of Washington, asked the questions and provided the guidance that led to this book. They deserve much of the credit for its strengths. Since I did not always understand the questions or follow the guidance, I take all responsibility for any weaknesses that remain.

Bill Silag and Gavin Lockwood of Iowa State University Press provided wise editorial support and direction. Jesse Dolch performed the unenviable but invaluable task of proofreading the book. I thank them for their contributions to this effort.

The support of the School of Journalism and the Freshman Seminars program at the University of Oregon contributed to the completion of the project.

The conversation, advice, and encouragement of Jeremy Cohen of Stanford University and Steve Ponder of the University of Oregon on questions ranging from legal analysis and historiography to the best way to negotiate Brown's Hole on the McKenzie River in a raft, deserves acknowledgment. Better colleagues and friends could not be found.

I met Jennifer Ulum, my wife, as I began this project. I am forever grateful to her for her understanding and encouragement throughout the research and writing of the book and for marrying me *after* going through the experience.

The Watchdog Concept

1

The Institutional Watchdog and Freedom of the Press

I N First Amendment theory and jurisprudence, freedom of speech and press is a right belonging to individuals. Justice Louis Brandeis captures the essence of this fundamental right in a classic statement of freedom of expression from *Whitney v. California*: "Those who won our independence believed that the final end of the state was to make men free to develop their faculties . . . They believed that freedom to think as you will and speak as you think are means indispensable to the discovery and spread of political truth."[1] In those two sentences, Brandeis identified two components of freedom of expression: the right of individuals to personal fulfillment through the exercise of freedom of expression and the right of individuals to participate in political debate. His sole emphasis on the individual's right without reference to government's power to limit that right reflects a twentieth-century concept of freedom of expression. Prior to the twentieth century, however, judges held a narrower view of the societal value of dissident speech.

In contrast to the liberal Brandeisian view of freedom of the press, nineteenth-century freedom of the press questions were resolved in the common law.[2] William Blackstone's defini-

tion illustrates the limited protections provided to freedom of
expression by the common-law view of freedom of the press:

> Every freeman has an undoubted right to lay what senti-
> ments he pleases before the public: to forbid this, is to
> destroy the freedom of the press: but if he publishes what
> is improper, mischievous, or illegal, he must take the con-
> sequences of his own temerity.[3]

Blackstone's definition of freedom of the press gave judges
broad discretionary power to determine the limits of proper expression. Rather than assuming the value of individual expression, the common law determined the value of expression by
measuring the public benefit of that expression. For readers
schooled in twentieth-century liberal free-press theory and constitutional law, the nineteenth-century balance between an individual's right to speak and the court's power to limit that right
for the public good may be a trip "through the looking glass"
where "things go the other way."[4]

In nineteenth-century libel law and contempt by publication case law, newspaper publishers raised the freedom of the
press as a barrier against unfavorable common-law doctrines.
Freedom of the press was not treated as a constitutional question, and the common law exposed a broad spectrum of newspaper content to libel or contempt actions. Within the common
law, publishers attempted to fashion a concept of freedom of
the press more favorable to the newspaper industry. In libel
litigation regarding the publication of matters of public concern, publishers argued that newspapers required special protections under the freedom of the press because the institution of
the press had a duty to gather and report information about the
operation of government and other matters of public interest.
They claimed that the press held unique newsgathering and news
disseminating abilities, therefore, a unique position in society;
that is, they claimed that the function of the institutional press
in society required that the law recognize an institutional right
to freedom of the press. This concept of freedom of the press is

now generally referred to as the "watchdog role of the press."[5]

In opposition to the nineteenth-century institutional claims for freedom of the press, twentieth-century liberal theorists have developed an individual-rights-based theory of freedom of the press. This effort has focused on the meaning of a free press within state and federal constitutional law.[6] Within these theories, legal scholars have attempted to incorporate both the individual's right to personal fulfillment and the right to participate in political debate into comprehensive theories of freedom of speech and press.[7] In recent years, legal theorists have participated in extensive dialogue about the theory and doctrine of freedom of expression.[8] Although significant differences exist among the participants of this debate, all agree that freedom of expression is an individual right and that any meaningful concept of freedom of speech and press must begin from that understanding.

But the watchdog concept also appears in free-press case law and discussions about the meaning of freedom of the press. Lawyers, judges, and commentators claim special protection for the institutional press. They argue that the institutional press has (or should have) special protection because of the societal function it serves as a gatherer and disseminator of information about the operation of government and other matters of public concern.[9]

Floyd Abrams, a prominent attorney who frequently represents media clients, has said that "the press is different" from any other institutional entity in the United States because "the press . . . serves as a vigilant protector of the public from its government."[10] And law professor Vincent Blasi suggests that "the inevitable size and complexity of modern government" creates the need for an institutional press "capable of acquiring enough information to pass judgment on the actions of government, and also capable of disseminating their information and judgments to the general public."[11]

The characterization of the press as a watchdog is also found in journalism literature. Journalism texts refer to the press as "the 4th Estate" and the press and reporters as "independent watchdogs," or "public servants."[12] A recent report on the public's view of the role of the press found that more than half of the people surveyed believed that "news organizations protect the democratic process," and sixty-seven percent believed the press "keeps political leaders from doing what should not be done." Halfway through President Ronald Reagan's first term *Columbia Journalism Review* asked, "Can our watchdog press sniff a smoking gun?" Clearly the watchdog is part of the American tradition of freedom of the press.[13]

Judicial recognition of the importance of the press's institutional function is firmly set in First Amendment case law. For example, in *Near v. Minnesota*, the first major freedom-of-the-press case decided by the Supreme Court of the United States, Chief Justice Charles Evans Hughes cited "the [public's] primary need of a vigilant and courageous press" to combat governmental "malfeasance and corruption."[14] In *Sheppard v. Maxwell*, Justice Tom Clark wrote, "The press . . . guards against the miscarriage of justice by subjecting the police, prosecutors, and judicial processes to extensive public scrutiny." Justice Hugo Black, in *New York Times v. United States*, rejected the government's claim of national security, writing that "the press was protected so that it could bare the secrets of government and inform the people." Finally, in *Saxbe v. Washington Post*, Justice Louis Powell called the press "an agent of the public at large."[15]

However, the general agreement and support for an institutional role for the press has not led to acceptance of the watchdog concept of freedom of the press. In 1980, following a term in which the Court heard several cases in which the press claimed "a distinct and preferred status," Archibald Cox observed that the "press has been notably unsuccessful in the effort to obtain special privileges and immunities."[16] Contrasting the liberal, individual-rights-based concept of freedom of the press to the watchdog concept suggests that theoretical inconsistency between the two concepts of freedom of the press contributes to the failure of the watchdog concept.

THE WATCHDOG AND FREE-PRESS THEORY

The watchdog concept is used by press advocates to lend support to claims of special constitutional protections for the press, but it is inconsistent with the twentieth-century liberal concept of freedom of the press. The right to freedom of the press is an individual right. The watchdog role of the press is based on the press's function as an institution serving a collective good. Instead of basing claims for greater protection on the individual rights of the reporters, editors, and publishers who make up the press, the watchdog attempts to establish a distinct institutional right. It is a complementary but different conception of the meaning of freedom of the press. Individual-based freedom of the press exists because individual expression has an inherent value to both the individual and to society. The watchdog role of the press is premised on the consequences of the institution's expression. Only the speech that benefits the collective good is worthy of protection.

Ronald Dworkin describes the watchdog concept as a "policy for free speech and free press"; that is, it is "intended to establish a collective goal." In contrast, the twentieth-century liberal concept of freedom of the press is a "principle of free speech": an individual right that protects "the historically central function of the First Amendment, which is simply to ensure that those who wish to speak on matters of political and social controversy are free to do so."

Dworkin argues that confusing the collective-based claim of the institutional press with the individual-based right weakens the power of the principle of freedom of speech and press. If judges decide free-press cases based on the principle of a fundamental human right to freedom of the press, the "right" should trump. However, if judges base free-press decisions on a policy of freedom of the press, they are less constrained by the individual right to freedom of the press and more likely to decide cases based on their perception of the public good.[17]

For example, in cases in which the press claimed a special right of access to prisons, the Supreme Court simply weighed the public benefit in granting the press special access against the government's assertion of the need for orderly and efficient operation of prisons. It found that orderly and efficient prisons served a greater public good.[18]

If the collective good is the primary criterion used to determine the meaning of the constitutional protection of freedom of the press, then constitutional free-press safeguards become less powerful. All Western democracies recognize freedom of the press, but, as becomes quite evident if the ability of government to regulate mass media freedom of the press in the United States is compared to the permissible regulation of media in England or other Western European countries, the constitutional right to freedom of the press in the United States is distinct. Aviam Soifer contrasts press law in the United States to press law in Western Europe and identifies the source and power of the right. "Freedom of the press in the United States is much more than a legal concept—it is almost a religious tenet . . . [T]he freedom of each citizen to communicate and to choose among diverse opinions is near the core of American individualism."[19]

In addition to Dworkin, a number of legal theorists and scholars argue that the watchdog concept is in conflict with the liberal, individual-right concept of freedom of the press. This position is stated in a number of ways, but a general statement of the argument contains the following elements:

(1) A rights-based concept of law only makes sense when discussed in terms of rights belonging to *individuals*. Under the federal Constitution only individuals (corporate entities are treated as individuals) can claim constitutional rights. This fundamental premise of the concept of rights and the clustering of

the constitutional right of freedom of the press with the freedoms of speech, religion, petition, and assembly embedded in a document specifically addressing individual rights are persuasive arguments against the claim that the First Amendment is an "unusual guarantee of [printers' and publishers'] business rights."[20]

(2) Traditional concepts of freedom of the press are based on a view of the press as a collection of individuals exercising an individual right and thereby serving the collective interest. For example, the "marketplace of ideas" theory of freedom of the press presumes that "the ultimate good desired is better reached through the fair trade of ideas."[21] Chafee defined the First Amendment as protecting two interdependent interests, both served by the exercise of an individual right of freedom of expression: "There is an individual interest, the need of many men to express their opinions on matters vital to them if life is to be worth living, and a social interest in the attainment of truth."[22]

(3) The watchdog concept assumes that the press is an institutional entity serving the collective good. If the measure of the institution's right to freedom of the press is its ability to serve the public interest, then the institution is not an independent entity exercising a right; it is subservient and has *legal* obligations to its public.

(4) Under the watchdog concept, the relation between the press and the public is one of "agency."[23] If the press is an agent of the people, it is accountable to standards set by the majority. Thus, the metaphor creates obligations and privileges for the press—not a unique right.

(5) The only sound basis for expanding or strengthening constitutional protection of the press is to fashion rationales based on the principle of freedom of the press. Authors have argued: that the *functions* of the press (e.g., newsgathering) should be protected when practiced by any individual; that the First Amendment exists to serve the value of "individual self-realization," which encompasses both political and nonpolitical speech; that "[u]nder the principle of freedom of expression

government is presumptively disabled from interfering with communication of or access to protected information or ideas . . . useful to the people in their allied capacities as participants in government and seekers of understanding"; and that principles of "autonomy" or "equality" best serve the interests of freedom of the press.[24]

THE ORIGIN OF THE WATCHDOG

The lack of a coherent watchdog concept within twentieth-century liberal free-press theory raises questions about the origin, development, and use of the watchdog concept in press law. If freedom of the press is an individual right — clearly the dominant view — then what is the source of the watchdog role of the press? How did it become part of a widely held tradition of freedom of the press?

One attempt to explain the watchdog concept focuses on status of the institutional press under the speech and press clauses of the First Amendment. Former Justice Potter Stewart advanced the thesis that the press clause is a structural provision of the Constitution.

> It is my thesis that . . . the established American press in the past ten years, has performed precisely the function it was intended to perform by those who wrote the First Amendment to our Constitution . . . [T]he free press guarantee is, in essence, a structural provision of the Constitution. . . . The publishing business is, in short, the only organized private business that is given explicit constitutional protection.[25]

Although Justice Stewart's thesis has attracted much attention, it has not been accepted by the Court.[26] And Anthony Lewis has suggested that Justice Stewart's use of both the speech and press clause in *Richmond Newspapers v. Virginia* was a "strategic withdrawal" from the idea of a special protection for the institutional press.[27]

Moreover, Stewart's thesis rests on shaky historical and theoretical grounds. Leonard Levy states that "the framers of the press clauses of the first state constitutions and of the first amendment could only have meant to protect the press as they knew it."[28] If this standard is applied to the press of the late 1700s, the nonexistence of an institutional press, as the phrase is understood in the late twentieth century, is shown.

Stephen Botein documents that "printers in pre-revolutionary times avoided controversy," and, for the most part, were "reluctant to advertise themselves as full-fledged partisans, many printers tried in public to claim the middle of the road."[29] Only about one-half of the printers operating in America published newspapers in 1775, and all printers needed job printing to survive financially. Much of their work consisted of printing broadsides and pamphlets for clients, and in most cases, the printers had no editorial influence on the content of the pamphlets.[30] Contrary to a watchdog role, Botein's study presents the press as being more like a common carrier than an institutional watchdog. Some printers were partisan and in opposition to the government, but the printing industry cannot be characterized as a watchdog.

Even though the press became more partisan during the American Revolution and remained so afterwards, its institutional function was very different from that described by Justice Stewart. Don Pember suggests that "the newspapers of that era . . . were papers of opinion and ideas . . . Newsgathering, reporting, access to government information as we speak of it today were not really an important part of the American press of that era."[31]

In one of a small number of attempts to provide historical support for Stewart's claim, David Anderson examined the history of the use of press clauses in "state constitutions and other declarations of the revolutionary period." Anderson demonstrates the frequent use of the words "liberty of the press" or similar phrasing, but, as Anderson states, he provides only a "history of the language."[32] The language by itself sheds little light on the question. Freedom of the press was an important right in the late eighteenth century, but writers used the words *speech* and *press* without making any clear distinction between the two.[33] The status, nature, and function of the colonial and revolutionary period press support an interpretation of freedom of the press as an extension of the individual's right of freedom of expression.

Because the watchdog is not consistent with the dominant individual-rights concept of freedom of the press and the Stewart thesis of special constitutional protection for the institution of the press does not survive scrutiny, another source for the watchdog concept must exist.

The common law was one such source. Newspaper publishers used the watchdog concept of freedom of the press as part of an extended effort to fashion special protection for newspapers in the common law of libel. The common law did not provide broad protection for individual speech. Judges had great freedom to determine the public good served by publication, and the measure of the public good defined the limits of protected speech. Publishers used the watchdog concept in an effort to create special protection in libel law for the press. They claimed that public journals had a special duty that mandated that they publish otherwise unprotected libels concerning public officials.

Until very recently historians of freedom of the press ignored the nineteenth century. The history of freedom of the press was the history of the First Amendment. Between the end of the Alien and Sedition Acts and the late 1800s, the federal government did not play a central role in regulating the press, and as a result few First Amendment cases were litigated before the twentieth century. However, freedom of the press was an important issue in nineteenth-century state courts. Examination of the use of the watchdog concept of freedom of the press sheds additional light on a largely ignored but very important segment of free-press history.

Moreover, it highlights the importance of legal process and practice in the development of free-press law. Traditional legal history focuses on the evolution of legal doctrine with little analysis of the social, political, or economic forces that influenced the law.[34] The development and use of the watchdog was not a result of doctrinal or theoretical changes in the law. It was the response of a special interest litigant to the demands of the common law.

The source of the watchdog concept is to be found in the practice of nineteenth-century common law, and this points out the tenuous relation between legal practice and legal theory. The law is a creature of the adversarial process. It is made in courtrooms in front of judges. Therefore, it is important to examine the practice of law in order to understand the product. But little sense can be made of the use and development of the watchdog concept without an understanding of free-press theory.

Harry Kalven, Jr., identifies the importance of this understanding in *The Negro and the First Amendment*. "[The search for First Amendment theory] presupposes agreement that the quest for a general theory in matters of the First Amendment needs no apology and no defense . . . free speech is so close to the heart of democratic organization that if we do not have an appropriate theory for our law here, we feel we really do not understand the society in which we live."[35] The ultimate goal in searching for the watchdog in nineteenth-century case law then is to contribute to the continuing effort to understand the meaning of freedom of the press in a democratic society.

In the remaining five chapters the use and development of the watchdog role of the press in nineteenth-century case law is explored. In looking for the watchdog concept, the relation between legal practice and theory, the importance of the adversarial system, and the influence of common law on the meaning of freedom of the press are identified as important factors in understanding the meaning of freedom of the press. Moreover, this study further demonstrates that, although free-press theory does not drive the development of press law, the two intersect.

2

Development of Free-Press Theory

WENTIETH-CENTURY efforts to shape the legal boundaries of freedom of the press frequently cite the writing of free-press theorists as part of attempts to persuade the audience of the correctness of a particular interpretation. But inserting an excerpt from the writing of, for example, John Milton or James Madison into a twentieth-century legal brief or court opinion tells us little about the philosophical or theoretical basis for freedom of expression.

Given the openness in the meaning of the phrase "freedom of the press" and the social, political, technological, and economic differences between seventeenth-century England and twentieth-century America, it is reasonable to assume that, for example, Milton had a different conception of the meaning of freedom of the press than the view held by a twentieth-century jurist in the United States. Yet twentieth-century judges and lawyers cite without qualification or clarification the words of Milton, Madison, John Stuart Mill, and others to support free-press arguments.

These same libertarian writers are cited to support twentieth-century free-press claims based on the watchdog concept of freedom of the press. Watchdog advocates argue that the traditional liberal free-press theory, which is based on a concept of freedom of the press as a right belonging to individuals, provides a conceptual framework for understanding freedom of the press as a right belonging to the press as an institution. The question explored in this chapter is whether or not individual-based liberal free-press theory contains or supports the watch-dog concept of freedom of the press.

An institutional right to freedom of the press, as it is defined in the watchdog concept, creates a unique constitutional niche for the mass media. If liberal free-press theory is to provide a conceptual basis for the watchdog concept, it must support the following claims:

(1) The press has a right to freedom of the press independent of the clearly recognized individual-based right. The independent basis for the right is critical. If liberal free-press theory does not provide a basis for a conceptualization of freedom of the institutional press distinct from the individual's right, then no conceptual basis exists for granting the institutional press greater freedom of the press.

(2) The press is entitled to greater free-press rights than the individual in the following areas: access to information, privileges of immunity when called to testify in a court of law or before other governmental investigatory bodies, immunities or privileges in libel law, and exemptions from injunctions.[1] Advocates advance the watchdog concept in support of claims for special protections in these areas.

At first glance the watchdog concept seems to be in agreement with liberal free-press theory. But careful examination of the development of liberal theory shows that early libertarian writers' conceptions of freedom of the press did not include any well-developed concept of a special independent status for the institutional press. They placed great emphasis on the concept of a watchdog public, but at best, only a hint of an institutional role for the press can be gleaned from early liberal theory. Moreover, none of the early theorists claimed that the institutional press had a special independent right to freedom of the press.

Establishing A Right to Freedom of the Press

The battle to establish a positive right to freedom of the press took place in the political domain. Political, religious, and economic concerns prompted calls for greater freedom of expression long before political philosophers explained its importance. Theoretical milestones in the early development of freedom of the press theory are few and far between. Milton's *Areopagitica* is generally considered the first major statement of an argument for freedom of the press based on a theory of freedom of expression. But Milton's powerful statement had little influence before the eighteenth century.[2]

In early sixteenth-century England, the king had complete authority to control and regulate the press. But during the century, questioning of fundamental religious and political beliefs changed both the political and religious structures of England and Europe. As the people began to assert and practice a right of religious and political discussion, the English Crown's regulation of printing was strained to the breaking point.[3]

Freedom of the press bloomed in the hothouse of seventeenth- and eighteenth-century English and European politics. As the people rejected the absolute authority of monarchical government and asserted rights of religious freedom and self-governance, freedom of the press became part of the bundle of fundamental natural rights that constituted liberty. It provided a means of education for the common man and thereby gave individual citizens the means to seek religious and political truth and to act as a powerful check on arbitrary use of governmental power.[4] In America, the influence of radical thinkers in Europe and England translated into what Bernard Bailyn has termed "a tradition of opposition."[5] American political thinkers and activists distrusted government. They assumed that government, if left unchecked, had a natural tendency to abridge the public's liberty. Freedom of the press gave the people a powerful weapon against the threat of government's abuse of its power.

In the political and religious turmoil of the time, few writers concerned themselves with determining a precise meaning for freedom of the press. Fredrick S. Siebert noted increasing violations of the English Crown's regulations on the press during the 1500s and, in the early 1600s, Puritan authors' protests against the Tudor's restrictions on their presses as well as efforts in Parliament to establish freedom of speech. But prior to *Areopagitica*, Siebert found only one conceptual argument for freedom of expression. Peter Wentworth, in a speech delivered in Parliament, argued that the pursuit of truth required freedom of discussion in Parliament. Wentworth's efforts landed him in prison.[6]

Leonard Levy found that "[t]he philosophical principle of freedom of the mind had merely a slight influence on the expansion of freedom of speech and press, at least through the eighteenth century." Though libertarian ideas about the freedom of the press were introduced in the eighteenth century, Levy found that "no one rejected the crux of the common law." Even Andrew Hamilton's famous defense of freedom of the press in the trial of John Peter Zenger, Levy noted, "was only slightly conceptual in character."[7]

By the end of the eighteenth century, the existence of a right to freedom of the press had been established in English and American law, but it was a limited positive right. In England, the common law definition of freedom of the press, as stated by Lord Mansfield, gave the government broad authority to punish those who exercised the right: "To be free is to live under a government by law. The liberty of the press consists in printing without any previous license, subject to the consequences of law."[8]

In the United States, the First Amendment to the Constitution of the United States, adopted in 1791, proscribed federal abridgment of freedom of the press. This amendment is of over-whelming significance because it signals the acceptance of freedom of the press as a prescriptive, fundamental right in a constitutional democracy; however, its adoption does not pro-vide a clear understanding of the meaning of freedom of the press. Although advocates of a more liberal view of freedom of the press argue that the authors of the First Amendment in-tended to establish constitutional protection for greater freedom of the press than the common law protected, the evidence is, at best, uncertain.

What is perhaps most surprising about the ongoing debate over the meaning of freedom of the press in the late 1700s is not the lack of a clearly defined meaning but rather the twentieth-century expectation that a well-developed concept of freedom of the press existed.[9] From the introduction of printing into England in the late fifteenth century to the adoption of the First Amendment in 1791, only a handful of writers attempted to develop a concept of freedom of the press.

FREE-PRESS THEORY TO THE NINETEENTH CENTURY

The establishment of freedom of the press as a positive right was a critical first step in the development of the right to freedom of the press, but in many ways it was the easier of two phases. The second phase—defining the meaning of the right—began in the seventeenth century and continues to occupy theorists, philosophers, lawyers, and other students of freedom of the press.

The second phase addresses two broad questions: (1) What is the value of an individual's expression in a society? (2) What criteria should judges use to interpret the meaning of existing constitutional, statutory, and common-law protections of freedom of the press? Liberal free-press theory begins with the assumption that freedom of the press is a fundamental right. It is fundamental because as human beings we must be allowed to seek the truth. Thus, the issue is not whether an individual has a right to freedom of the press; it is determining the power of government to limit that right.

No right or freedom in a society is an absolute. At some point the exercise of any right interferes with the freedom of another individual. Not infrequently, the exercise of an individual right may appear to be in conflict with the interests of the society. If three individuals gather to exchange ideas and all three speak at once or one of the three refuses to let the other two speak, or if another of the three uses his right to freedom of the press to provide false information or to use language that the other two find offensive, the conversation will not be productive. It is likely that the three individuals will develop some rules that will limit each person's right to freedom of speech in order to create a system in which the collective interest in a productive conversation is served. When the process of developing rules for communication is expanded to a societal scale, government serves as the rulemaker. Government attempts to develop rules that achieve a proper balance between the individual's rights and the collective interests of the society. The question of freedom of the press becomes one of weighing the individual's right to freedom of the press against government's perception of the public interest in the exercise of the individual right to freedom of the press.[10]

Milton and Locke

The writings of John Milton and John Locke had a major influence on the development of liberal free-press theory. Both argued against government licensing of the press but also accepted and even encouraged other forms of governmental restraint on the individual's right to freedom of the press. Neither Milton nor Locke suggested a watchdog concept. They were concerned with the individual's right to freely seek the truth through discussion of a relatively narrow spectrum of ideas and opinions.

Milton's *Areopagitica* is the seminal work in support of freedom of expression. He presented the first reasoned argument for the idea that freedom of expression served the public good. His writing is important because it was the first and because it influenced later theorists. However, Milton's contemporaries ignored *Areopagitica* and his concept of freedom of the press was much less libertarian than many would like to admit.

Milton wrote *Areopagitica* after he was admonished for printing an unlicensed essay in support of liberal divorce laws.[11] In calling for "Liberty of Unlicensed Printing," Milton did not distinguish freedom of the press from the broader concept of freedom of expression. The press was an extension of man's ability to think and express his thoughts. In arguing for the futility of licensing as a way to stop the spread of ideas, he asked, "And who shall silence all the airs and madrigals that whisper softness in chambers?"[12]

Milton focused on freedom of the press rather than a general right of freedom of expression because government could and did license printing. The search for truth through the use of speech and press formed the basis of the right.

Milton opposed licensing of the press, but his concept of freedom of the press was quite limited. Levy suggests that "in all likelihood Milton never intended that anything but the serious works of intellectuals, chiefly scholars and Protestant divines should be really free."[13]

Two brief passages from Milton's argument in favor of freedom of expression are commonly quoted. Both, if taken out of context, stand as broad statements of the public good served by protection of the individual right of freedom of expression:

> Ye cannot make us now less capable, less knowing, less eagerly pursuing of the truth, unless ye first make yourselves, that made us so, less the lovers, less the founders of our true liberty . . . Give me the liberty to know, to utter, and to argue freely according to conscience, above all liberties.
>
> And though all the winds of doctrine were let loose to play upon the earth, so Truth be in the field, we do inju-

riously by licensing and prohibiting to misdoubt her strength. Let her and Falsehood grapple; who ever knew Truth put to the worse, in a free and open encounter? Her confuting is the best and surest suppressing.[14]

Milton believed that freedom of the press served the search for truth, but once truth had been discovered, falsehood should be suppressed. Licensing interfered with the search for truth, but punishment of falsehood was to be encouraged. He protested the "incredible loss and detriment that this plot of licensing puts us to" as a barrier to the search for truth. But he supported mandatory registration of printed material and punishment after the fact: "Those which otherwise come forth, if they are found mischievous and libelous [sic], the fire and the executioner will be the timeliest and most effectual remedy that mans' prevention can use."[15]

In Milton's view, freedom of the press was far from an absolute right. An individual exercised the right to freedom of the press only as long as his expression contributed to the search for truth; all other speech threatened the public interest and therefore fell outside the narrow area of protected expression.

From Milton's writing in 1644 until the adoption of the First Amendment in 1791, this narrow view of the meaning of freedom of the press prevailed. Authors recognized the right to seek truth through rational discussion of ideas, but even the most libertarian writers accepted broad government authority to punish speech that threatened the public good.

This concept of public interest is critical to an understanding of the development of freedom-of-the-press theory. Freedom of the press existed to enable man to search for truth. But it did not create a right to threaten the public good or disrupt the social order. Falsehood, blasphemy, scandal, or any other speech deemed a threat to the public good fell outside the natural right to freedom of the press.

John Locke, whose writings had great influence on political thinking in the American colonies, opposed government licensing of the press, but like Milton, Locke called for far less than absolute freedom of the press.[16] He opposed government licensing because it interfered with the creation of the diversity of opinion necessary for the pursuit of truth in a society. However, Locke drew a small circle around protected speech and called for prosecution of expression that threatened the proper social order: "[N]o opinions contrary to human society or to those moral rules which are necessary to the preservation of civil society, are to be tolerated by the magistrate."[17]

Locke, and other libertarian writers of the seventeenth and eighteenth centuries, saw no conflict between freedom of the press and government prosecution of wide areas of expression. These early conceptualizations of the individual's right to freedom of expression as protecting only speech that served society's interests not only established the need for protection of a diversity of opinion but also set the public good as the primary criterion for determining the limits of freedom of the press.

The practice of freedom of the press in America during the seventeenth and eighteenth centuries demonstrated the broad public support for the individual's right to publish criticism of government. However, the existing legal authority to punish publishers of seditious libel, blasphemy, obscenity, and other expression considered a threat to the public good and liberal support of this use of governmental power indicate general support for a concept of freedom of the press that included the proper use of governmental power to punish expression threatening to the public interest. The issue debated in the late 1700s centered on the kinds of expression the government could regulate to serve the public interest.[18]

Licensing or any other form of prior restraint (that is, any governmental authority to prohibit publication before the fact) violated freedom of the press because prior restraints completely destroy the individual's fundamental right to express and receive competing ideas and opinions. Other forms of restraint that take place after the fact, such as prosecutions for libel or blasphemy, allow the people to compare competing ideas and reach decisions about the value of ideas. Once the people had determined what speech was true and therefore served the public good, none of the early free-press advocates questioned government's responsibility and authority to punish speakers or printers of falsehoods. This view of government's role in regulating expression placed the focus of discussion about freedom of the press on the issue that fueled the use of freedom of the press as a rallying cry in eighteenth-century America and still occupies center stage in liberal free-press theory.

Opposition Ideology

In the 1700s, English radicals "insisted," Bernard Bailyn wrote, "that [the power of the state] was necessarily—by its very nature—hostile to human liberty and happiness."[19] This distrust of government created an adversarial relationship between the government and the people. Within the context of an adversarial relationship, freedom of the press gave the people a weapon in the battle to protect individual liberty from governmental abuse.

The value of freedom of the press as a means of combating what eighteenth-century men in America viewed as an inevitable condition—the abuse of governmental power—is the core of the dominant theory of freedom of the press in America at the time of the adoption of the First Amendment to the Constitution of the United States and state constitutional free-press clauses.

Freedom of the press was an important fundamental right because it served as a means of stopping governmental abuse of power. The press provided the public the means to discover, organize, and fight governmental abuse; the power of public opinion provided an influential check on governmental use of power. This adversarial relationship between the people and the government and the checking value of freedom of the press were the primary components of "opposition ideology."[20]

Two extreme radical English pamphleteers, John Trenchard and Thomas Gordon, had a significant influence on American political thought in the early to mid-1700s. Writing under the name Cato, their political commentary appeared in newspapers and pamphlets throughout the colonies. The political theory espoused by Cato found its source in the "radical social and political thought of the English Civil War and of the Commonwealth period" of the late 1600s. It was a radical "tradition of opposition" based on a distrust of unchecked governmental power.[21] Richard Buel describes it as an "opposition ideology" premised on "a theory of politics postulating that the basic problem in government was how to establish an equilibrium between two forces, one tending to destroy liberty, the other to defend it."[22]

The right to freedom of expression played a central role in creating a balance between the government and the people. Cato frequently wrote about freedom of speech and press, and the collected works indicate the blending of a natural right theory of freedom of expression with opposition ideology. In "Of Freedom Of Speech," Cato identified this natural right basis for freedom of expression:

> Without freedom of Thought, there can be no such thing as Wisdom; and no such thing as publick Liberty, without Freedom of Speech: Which is the right of every Man, as far as by it he does not hurt and controul the Right of another.

He then stated the checking value of freedom of expression:

> That Men ought to speak well of their Governors, is true, while their Governors deserve to be well spoken of; but to do publick Mischief, without hearing of it, is only the Prerogative and Felicity of Tyranny; A free People will be shewing that they are so, by their freedom of speech. . . . Only the wicked Governors of Men dread what is said about them.[23]

The checking value of freedom of the press was of paramount importance because it gave the public a means of stopping governmental wrongdoing. Any government action that inhibited the checking value was a violation of freedom of the press.

The liberal argument against seditious libels, Cato stated, was government's authority to punish individuals who criticized the government. This violated freedom of the press because the *public* had the right and responsibility to act as a watchdog. "The exposing therefore of publick wickedness, as it is a Duty which every man owes to Truth and his Country, can never be a Libel in the Nature of Things."[24] Cato and other liberal free-press advocates argued that the public benefits of the checking value of freedom of the press outweighed the evils of the abuse of freedom of the press. "[T]o shut up the Press because it has been abused," William Livingston wrote in 1753, "would be like burning our Bibles and proscribing Religion, because its Doctrines have been disobeyed and misrepresented."[25]

But Livingston did not claim that all criticism of government fell under the protection of freedom of the press. Freedom of the press was, he wrote, "a Liberty of promoting the common Good of Society, and of publishing any Thing else not repugnant thereto."[26] Opposition ideology assumed government would act against the public good, and that the checking value of freedom of the press gave individuals a weapon for the protection of the public good.

Opposition ideology shaped the eighteenth-century view of freedom of the press in America. When Cato, Samuel Adams, or the other revolutionary period champions of a free press spoke of freedom of the press as being a "bulwark of liberty," they were talking about the peoples' use of the press, not about an institutional press. Levy suggests that the concept of a public watchdog found in *Cato's Letters* "led ultimately, to a theory of the press as the 'fourth estate,' a watchdog of government on behalf of the people." And indeed, the newspaper industry in the nineteenth century took the concept of a watchdog public found in opposition ideology and used it to fashion its own institutional watchdog concept of freedom of the press. But when the states and the federal government adopted free-press guarantees in the late eighteenth and early nineteenth centuries, the concept of an institutional watchdog had not been developed. The lack of any notion of an institutional watchdog role for the press in early theory suggests that the all-too-often cited view of the First Amendment as a "unique guarantee of [publishers'] business rights" is a significant departure from free-press theory as it had developed by the late 1700s.[27]

In the last years of the eighteenth century and the first years of the nineteenth century, the enactment of the Alien and Sedition Acts generated the most concentrated discussion of the meaning of freedom of the press prior to the twentieth century. In the liberal response to the Federalist Congress's sedition statute, Jeffersonian Republicans fashioned a liberal concept of the freedom of the press built on the liberal tradition of Milton, Locke, and opposition ideology.

The Virginia Report of 1799–1800

The Alien and Sedition Acts, enacted in 1798, generated a constitutional crisis and the first sustained effort to articulate a liberal theory of freedom of the press in a constitutional democracy. The Sedition Act gave the executive the power to bring criminal prosecutions for seditious libel against anyone who libeled the president of the United States, the members of his cabinet, or members of Congress.

Seventeenth-century libertarian writers had fashioned an argument against seditious libel within the context of opposition ideology. But one of the fundamental assumptions of opposition ideology—an adversarial relationship between the government and the people—was no longer certain. The Sedition Act had been passed by a government elected by the people to protect the public interest.

Because a duly elected representative Congress enacted the law, a new and more complex question confronted those who believed it violated the freedom of the press. Clearly, the First

Amendment proscribed prior restraints or legislation giving the federal government arbitrary power to punish speech. But did freedom of the press prevent an elected representative government from passing legislation intended to protect the people's government from criticism it believed threatened the viability of that government? The Federalist government asserted its right and duty to protect the public interest and preserve the government. The Jefferson-led opposition disagreed.[28]

The Virginia Legislature appointed a committee headed by James Madison to prepare a report opposing the act.[29] The report contained two themes that provided the basis for more elaborate discussions of liberal free-press theory in the early 1800s.

In one of the most quoted passages in the free-press pantheon, Madison balanced the licentiousness of the press against the public good served by its checking value and found the checking value outweighed the evils of the press.

> It has accordingly been decided by the practice of the states, that it is better to leave a few of the noxious branches to their luxuriant growth, than by pruning them away, to injure the vigour of those yielding the proper fruit. And can this wisdom be doubted by any who reflect, that to the press alone, chequered as it is with abuses, the world is indebted for all the triumphs which have been gained by reason and humanity, over error and oppression.

Freedom of the press led to some abuses, but Madison argued that only the "strictures of the press" forced government officials to meet the responsibilities of office.[30]

Clearly, Madison is talking about "the press" in institutional terms. He was not referring to printing presses randomly scattered around the country, but neither is he clearly defining an independent role for an institutional press. The press to which Madison referred consisted of partisan political newspapers that were extensions of the political parties of the day.

Party newspapers were the means by which participants in political debate broadcast their views.[31]

Madison looked to the demands of a representative constitutional government and found freedom of the press to be an essential component. He believed that

> the right of electing the members of the government, constitutes more particularly the essence of free and responsible government. The value and efficacy of this right, depends on the knowledge of the comparative merits and demerits of the candidates respectively . . . and free communication thereon, is the only effectual guardian of every other right.[32]

The Virginia Report emphasized the checking value of freedom of the press and the press's function as a means of disseminating information. These two themes form the basis for the later development in case law of the watchdog role of the press.

As writers who followed Madison made clear, the libertarian tradition of freedom of the press recognized the importance of an institutional press as part of a watchdog public, but it did not carve out the special niche for the institutional press found in the watchdog concept of freedom of the press.

LIBERTARIAN THOUGHT IN THE NINETEENTH CENTURY

The Alien and Sedition Act crisis of 1798 to 1801 demonstrated the lack of either a well-articulated theory of freedom of the press or a clear consensus about the legal boundaries of freedom of expression following the adoption of the First Amendment. In the first few years of the nineteenth century, liberal political writers supported a concept of freedom of the press broader than the Blackstonian definition of freedom of the press.

In an essay published in 1800, Tunis Wortman, a Jeffersonian Republican and a New York attorney, argued for a liberal
concept of freedom of the press. His essay contained the main
themes presented throughout the nineteenth century by advocates of a liberal concept of freedom of the press and suggested
an institutional role for the press.[33] Wortman's discussion is
carefully reasoned and goes far beyond the specific issue of the
constitutionality of the Alien and Sedition laws.

For Wortman, the question of freedom of the press concerned the nature of representative government. In the republican form of government established by the Constitution of the
United States, Wortman wrote, "The government of the United
States is the genuine offspring of a pre-existing determination of
public volition. . . . With respect to government, therefore,
everything is dependent upon the public will." Given the importance of public opinion, he reasoned, "it should therefore be
established as an essential principle, that freedom of investigation is one of the most important rights of a people."[34]

Wortman's view of the checking value of freedom of the
press contained the legacy of opposition ideology. "Society," he
said, "should incessantly maintain a species of censorial jurisdiction over its political institution." If the public did not have the
knowledge necessary to act as an effective check on government,
Wortman saw only one means of correcting the abuses of government—violent action. "The history of mankind, so pregnant
with vicissitudes, must convince us that revolutions and inten-
sive commotions, have invariably proceeded from the abuse of
power."[35]

Having established a basis for the public's right to investigate the operation of government, Wortman turned to the question of the societal benefit of the press.

> While Society is furnished with so powerful a vehicle of
> Political Information [as the press], the conduct of ad-
> ministration will be more cautious and deliberate; it will be
> inspired with respect towards a Censor whose influence is

universal. Ambition cannot fail to dread that vigilant
guardian of Public Liberty, whose eye can penetrate, and
whose voice be heard, in every quarter of the State. . . .
The Press is, therefore, an excellent auxiliary to promote
the progressive perfection of the Representative System.[36]

Wortman described the press as an institution with a societal role. The press served the public good by providing citizens with the information they needed to function as an effective
watchdog public. He did not say that the press was an independent institution with extraordinary rights or status; rather, he
placed the press in a position subservient to the public interest.
Wortman, just as earlier libertarian writers, defined the limits of
freedom of the press in terms of the public good. The public was
the watchdog and the press functioned as an information provider serving the public's interest.

Wortman feared the abuse of governmental power, but he
also feared the abuse of the power of the press. The "extensive
influence" of the press required, he said, that "every exertion
should . . . be employed to render it subservient to Liberty,
Truth, and Virtue."[37]

Seditious libel violated the freedom of the press because, he
argued, representative democracy demanded that room exist for
error in the discussion of public officials and candidates. The
amount of discussion necessary for proper decision making in a
democracy inevitably leads to mistakes, but, he wrote, "public
prosecution in such cases will be always liable for abuse: it will
infallibly be made a tremendous weapon in the hands of officers
of the state to oppress and intimidate the people."[38]

However, Wortman did not suggest that private libels — that
is, false malicious statements about the private life of a private
person or a public official — should be protected by the freedom
of the press. In that he defined freedom of the press in terms of
the public interest in discussing and examining public matters,
he had no difficulty distinguishing private libels from public
libels. Private libels served no public interest and no conflict

existed between civil libel actions based on private libels and the freedom of the press.[39]

Wortman's conceptualization of freedom of the press centered on its value to individuals in a representative government. His view of the relationship between government and the people is pure opposition ideology—if the people do not check the use of power, public officials *will* abuse governmental powers. The watchdog public needed an institutional press as a means of distributing information, but the press was subservient to the public. Wortman seems to distrust unchecked power of the press only slightly less than an unchecked government.

Clearly, power concentrated in *any* hands, except the people's, concerned Wortman. Although he frequently used the language of natural rights (for example, "There is no natural right more perfect or more absolute, than that of investigating every subject which concerns us"), the strong basis for Wortman's conception of freedom of the press was its instrumental value as a check on government power.[40] Expression that did not serve the public's need for information about public matters fell outside the protection of freedom of the press.

Wortman's treatise disappeared shortly after it was written. Its primary value is that it illuminates the importance of the checking value of freedom of the press in the early nineteenth-century liberal concept of freedom of the press. In contrast, St. George Tucker's discussion of freedom of the press in his edition of *Blackstone's Commentaries,* published in 1803, became a primary legal source and authority in the early nineteenth century. Tucker's interpretation of a free press supported and in parts echoed The Virginia Report and Wortman's essay.[41]

Tucker presented a much broader definition of the liberty of speech and press than Blackstone:

> Liberty of speech and discussion in all speculative matters, consists in the absolute and uncontrollable right of speaking, writing, and publishing our opinions concerning any subject . . . and of inquiry into and examining, the nature

of truth . . . the expediency or inexpediency of all public
measures, with their tendency and probable effect; the conduct of public men, and generally every other subject,
without restraint, except as to the injury of any other individual, in his person, property, or good name.[42]

The press, Tucker said, provided a means for preserving
ideas. Because speech is transitory, open to rapid and inaccurate
interpretation, and frequently influenced by the passions of the
moment, "the only adequate supplementary aid for those defects is the absolute freedom of the press." The written word
allowed the reader to pause and reflect upon the ideas presented
and to return to them time and again. The "security of freedom
of the press," he wrote, "requires that it should be exempt, not
only from previous restraint by the executive . . . but from legislative restraint also; and this exemption, to be effectual, must
be an exemption, not only from previous inspection of licensers,
but from the subsequent penalty of laws."[43]

However, freedom of the press did not extend to licentious
publications that did not serve the public interest.

A free press, conducted with ability, firmness, decorum,
and impartiality, may be regarded as the chaste nursemaid
of genuine liberty; but a press stained with falsehood, im-
posture, detraction, and personal slander resembles a con-
taminated prostitute, whose touch is pollution and whose
offspring bears the foul marks of the parent's ignominy.

The First Amendment stopped the federal government from
passing laws allowing prosecution for libels against the character of a public official, but Tucker observed that "the state courts
are always open, and may afford ample, and competent redress,
as the records of the courts and this commonwealth abundantly
testify."[44]

After the Jeffersonian Republicans' concentrated response
to the Sedition Act, few nineteenth-century Americans took the
time to write about theories of freedom of the press. One ob-

server wrote in 1841 that Americans "lived in the rich experience
and practical enjoyment of democratic freedom, but in entire
and reckless indifference to its abstract principles."[45]

Thomas Cooper's *A Treatise on the Law of Libel and the
Liberty of the Press* is one of a few extended discussions of
freedom of the press after the Sedition Act period. Cooper's
treatment benefited from the interlude between his prosecution
under the Sedition Act and its publication, but it must be viewed
as a final shot in the battle over the Sedition Act.[46]

Cooper followed in the liberal tradition of seeking truth
through the competition of ideas. The most effective means for
battling error, he said, was to "publish it, expose it, discuss it,
and the vapor is dissipated before the beams of truth." But
because he measured the boundaries of freedom of the press by
the public interest served by the information published, he saw
no tensions between civil libel and freedom of the press: "[The]
tendency toward calumny toward neighbors, ought to be re-
pressed."[47]

> Where the public are not interested, a needless exposure of
> those frailties can never be made from a praiseworthy mo-
> tive. . . . I would therefore consider freedom of discussion
> and the liberty of the press, as relating to questions of
> general and public nature only; and where the discussion is
> expedient to elicit a truth proper for the public to know.[48]

Cooper's discussion of government's power to regulate expression that might lead to undesirable actions was his most
important contribution to the theory of freedom of the press.
Cooper presented a strong argument against the use of "bad
tendency tests." Freedom of the press, he said, stood for the
proposition that "speculative opinions are best left to fight out
their own harmless battles by means of a free press. They are
not dangerous to the community but when the magistrates take
sides." The proper role of government, Cooper argued, was to
"let the laws regulate our *actions*, which are within the power of

regulation; and leave our *opinions* alone, because no external force can produce or destroy them."[49]

Wortman, Tucker, and Cooper are representative of the liberal voice in the discussion over the meaning of freedom of the press in the nineteenth century. While the concepts of freedom of expression found in their writings differ from the existing common law as to the proper limits of freedom of the press, the concepts are similar to the prevailing view of the public good as the sole basis for determining the limits of freedom of the press. Freedom of the press ended when expression no longer served the dominant concept of the public's interest. To the middle of the nineteenth century, no one had suggested that speech in and of itself, regardless of its perceived public value, deserved protection. Madison, Wortman, and Tucker had discussed the press in institutional terms and recognized its important role as a disseminator of information to the watchdog public. But none of the important advocates of a liberal concept of freedom of the press had attempted to develop a distinct institutional watchdog concept of freedom of the press.

John Stuart Mill

For twentieth-century students of free-press theory, John S. Mill's *On Liberty* is a most important nineteenth-century treatment of freedom of the press. Mill expanded the liberal tradition of Milton and Locke into a broader concept of freedom of the press. His conception of freedom of the press had little impact on the legal definition of freedom of the press at the time, but it was the theoretical foundation for the development of the twentieth-century concept of freedom of the press.[50]

Mill embedded his concept of freedom of the press in his view of individual liberty. The first component of human liberty is, Mill wrote, "the inward domain of consciousness; demanding liberty of consciousness in the most comprehensive sense; liberty of thought and feeling; absolute freedom of opinion and senti-ment on all subjects, practical or speculative, scientific, moral, or theological." Freedom of the press derived from this first component of individual liberty because it "rest[ed] in great part on the same reasons" and was "practically inseparable" from freedom of thought.[51]

Mill's emphasis on the relation of freedom of the press to freedom of thought and discussion raised an important issue in examining the relation between the watchdog role of the press as used and defined by advocates of the newspaper industry and Millian theory. Throughout *On Liberty*, Mill referred to the lib-erty to publish "opinions." His view of freedom of the press is premised on the use of the freedom to advance the rational and reasoned discussion of matters of importance to individual members of society. His essay concerned, Mill said, "liberty of thought, from which it is impossible to separate the cognate liberty of speaking and writing."[52]

He is concerned with the protection of minority ideas from the tyranny of the majority. Minority views, even those opinions held by a minority of one, must be protected from government restriction because it is possible that one person may offer un-known, partial, or whole truths that may be of value to individ-uals or that exposure to false opinions or doctrines will aid individuals in the search for truth.[53]

Mill provided a philosophical argument for the protection of false ideas, but his emphasis on the search for truth and the importance of protection of opinion lends little support to argu-ments that freedom of the press requires the protection of false statement of fact. How, one can ask, is the search for truth advanced by the publication of easily determined erroneous facts? What individual's pursuit of happiness or pleasure will be aided by a false report of an arrest or a good faith publication of a malicious lie about a candidate for office?

Mill's view of the limited role of government in the affairs of individual citizens, not his view of the value of speech, pro-vided support for protection of false statements of fact. The history of government regulation of the press showed that most government regulation was designed to protect the interests of government, not the interests of the individual citizen, therefore, government regulation of the press should be limited to situations in which a clear threat to the public interest in public order and safety government action.

> An opinion that corn-dealers are starvers of the poor, or that private property is robbery, ought to be unmolested when simply circulated through the press, but may incur punishment when delivered orally to an excited mob assembled before the house of a corn-dealer, or when handed about among the same mob in the form of a placard.

Restraint before an incitement to violence existed, he said, "would have an ill effect on the moral nature of man." For this reason, the restraint of "intemperate discussion, namely invective, sarcasm, personality, and the like" should be left to public opinion.[54]

Mill, like Milton, had a greater impact on the concept of freedom of the press in the century after he wrote than he did on contemporary debate. Nineteenth-century jurists and advocates for freedom of the press did not cite Mill or any other philosopher or theorist. They relied on the common law and judicially determined measures of the public good to find intemperate, inaccurate, or false speech to be outside the limits of freedom of the press.

Zechariah Chafee's *Freedom of Speech* became the first milestone in the modern history of free-press theory. Chafee, and those who followed, ignored or dismissed as misguided most of the nineteenth-century history of press freedom and instead created a liberal tradition that drew from Mill and the American tradition of freedom of the press.

> Into the making of the constitutional conception of free speech have gone, not only men's bitter experience of the censorship and sedition prosecutions before 1791, but also the subsequent development of the law of fair comment in

civil defamation, and the philosophical speculations of
John Stuart Mill.[55]

By ignoring a substantial body of legal history that supported a concept of freedom of the press based on government's
power to regulate speech to serve majoritarian interests and by
carefully choosing language from liberal free-press theorists,
Chafee created a foundation for the development of a free-press
theory based on the inherent value of expression and the public
good in the protection of individual speakers from the tyranny
of the majority. Since Chafee published *Freedom of Speech,* a
large body of free-press literature has developed. For the most
part, the history of freedom of the press in the nineteenth century has not been a part of twentieth-century free-press thinking.

But the watchdog concept of freedom of the press, which is
a part of twentieth-century free-press literature, existed in the
nineteenth century. This chapter has shown that until the beginning of the twentieth century, liberal free-press theory contained
a strong concept of a watchdog public, but no statement of
special protection for the institutional press. In order to find the
origins of the watchdog, we must look to the practice of law in
the nineteenth century.

CHAPTER

3

Law in the Nineteenth Century

UDGE Thomas Cooley, one of the most influential jurists and legal scholars of the nineteenth century, instructed lawyers and jurists to "look to the common law for the meaning of freedom of the press." "At the common law," he observed, "it will be found that the liberty of the press was neither well protected nor well defined."[1]

Cooley's focus on the common law as the source of understanding freedom of the press seems strange to late twentieth-century readers accustomed to thinking of freedom of the press as a constitutional question. But nineteenth-century jurists, lawyers, and litigants relied on the principles and practices of the common law — not constitutional law — in efforts to define and shape the meaning of freedom of the press. Newspaper advocates and judges cited state constitutional free-press clauses and language, but constitutional protection of freedom of the press did little more than color the common law. At the end of the nineteenth century, Alexander Hamilton's common law interpretation of the freedom of the press, put forth in *People v. Croswell*, remained the dominant view of the meaning of freedom of the press. Freedom of the press, he said, "consists in the right to publish, with impunity, truth, with good motives, for justifiable ends, though reflecting on government, magistracy, or individuals."[2]

39

Within the common law, uncertainty over the limits of protected expression centered on determination of "good motives"
and "justifiable ends." When confronted with claims of violations of freedom of the press, judges weighed the motives of the
publisher and the public value of the expression. Journalists
frequently raised the freedom of the press as a defense in litigation, but the common-law conception of freedom of the press
protected a limited range of expression and it bears little re-
semblance to twentieth-century constitutional freedom of the
press.

A second major difference between nineteenth- and twentieth-century treatment of freedom of the press is the nature of
nineteenth-century legal training and scholarship. An aspiring
attorney could take one of three roads to the bar: (1) He could
clerk in a private law office, (2) self-educate himself in the law
by reading legal treatises, (3) attend law school.[3]

For most of the century, the vast majority of practicing
lawyers prepared for the bar by clerking in private firms or
through self-education. Law schools became an increasingly important influence in legal education after the Civil War, but at
the end of the century about one-third of the lawyers admitted
to the bar lacked a formal legal education.[4]

Law schools offered a more structured legal education, but
all three types of legal training offered a practical view of the
law. The task was to learn the law, not to think about the meaning of the law. The sole emphasis in legal education on what is
generally referred to as "black letter law" contributed to a pragmatic, narrow, technical approach to legal practice.[5]

A third difference between nineteenth- and twentieth-century legal thinking is the relation of individual rights to the
public interest. Nineteenth-century law protected the interests of
the majority and placed little emphasis on the protection of
individual minority interests. Judges viewed the law as an instrument for the protection of majority values and interests. The
perceived interests of the majority defined the proper ends of
freedom of the press when judges attempted to determine what

constituted justifiable expression. Christopher Tiedeman described the dominance of majority interests over an individual's right to freedom of the press in the following manner.

> The tendency of the press, at least in this country, is to publish sensational, and often false accounts in individual wrongs and immoralities, to such an extent that newspapers too often fall properly within the definition of obscene literature. If possible, the publication of such literature should be suppressed, or at least published in such a way, as to do little harm to the morals of the community.[6]

During the nineteenth century, state legislatures and the Congress passed numerous laws to restrain publications for the stated purpose of protecting social, political, and moral values. Most of these measures withstood legal challenges based, in part, on claims of freedom of the press.[7]

This chapter gives an overview of nineteenth-century law as it pertained to freedom of the press. Three topics are discussed: the common law, the teaching and scholarship of law, and the use of law to protect majoritarian interests. Finally, this chapter provides the necessary background for analysis of the development of the watchdog role of the press in nineteenth-century libel case law.

THE COMMON LAW

The common law is "judge made law . . . that has its origins in England and grows from ever-changing custom and tradition."[8] In the nineteenth century, judges struggled to adapt English common law to the realities and problems of American society. Early nineteenth-century judges looked to the English common law to support interpretations of state constitutional freedom of the press clauses. By the 1820s, judges acknowledged the importance of constitutional protection of freedom of the press as an influence on the common law, but the rules and conventions of the common law remained the dominant legal influence on the definition of freedom of the press. As a body of American common law developed, judges began to rely on American precedent to support their decisions, but in some areas of law, most notably the law of libel, English precedents are cited throughout the nineteenth century. The continued reliance on English case law suggests the relative lack of importance placed on constitutional protections of freedom of the press in most nineteenth-century courtrooms. Judges recognized constitutional protections, but looked to the English common law to determine the meaning and extent of the protection provided under the constitution.

Two aspects of the growth of American common law that are important to this study are (1) the judicial role as legislator within the constraints of the common law, and (2) the use of motive and justification within an "instrumental conception of law."[9]

The common law is never static. Judges must pay attention to the body of case law pertaining to the issue before the bench, but precedent is "persuasive . . . not conclusive." In response to the social, political, and economic issues brought into state courts in the nineteenth century, judges developed new precedent. It is clear that judges used the common law to shape public policy. Jurists shaped the law to achieve results that reflected their views of the public interest.[10]

The common-law definition of freedom of the press qualified by "good motives" and "justifiable intent" gave judges broad discretion to determine what types of expression were protected under the freedom of the press. Judges did not consider the inherent value of expression, but rather used the criteria of motive and justification to determine the value of expression as a means to achieve certain public policy goals. Throughout the century, judges found that licentious, libelous, immoral, obscene, or sensational publications served no public interest and therefore fell outside the protection of freedom of the press.[11]

The watchdog concept addressed the criteria of good motive and justifiable intent. Had the judiciary been willing to accept publishers' claims that the newspaper industry had a *duty* to the public that required it to publish otherwise unprotected expression, the watchdog function would have satisfied the criteria of good motive and justifiable intent. But judges proved unreceptive to the claim of a watchdog role for the press and continued to treat the press and the public alike under the constrained common-law definition of freedom of the press.

LEGAL TRAINING

Nineteenth-century lawyers were the products of what legal historian Willard Hurst said was "a limited, and wholly technical, conception of training for the bar."[12] Certainly the nineteenth century produced its share of great legal minds, but the training of lawyers and the vast bulk of legal scholarship consisted of narrow, legalistic expositions of the existing legal principles with little or no discussion of conceptual or theoretical concerns.

As late as 1900, admission to the bar required neither a college degree nor a law degree. During much of the nineteenth century, a majority of lawyers prepared for the bar by clerking in a private law office or reading St. George Tucker's American edition of *Blackstone's Commentaries* and the small number of other available legal treatises and then taking a bar exam. Hurst described this method of preparation for the practice of law as being "narrow technical training out of a few ill-assorted books." The average self-trained or apprenticed lawyer had little knowledge of the law outside the jurisdiction in which he trained and even less knowledge of legal principles or theory.[13]

University law schools became the preferred path to a law career after the Civil War. But the law schools of the late nineteenth century did little to expand the narrow technical, legalistic focus of nineteenth-century legal training. Law professors, first using the textbook method and later the case-book method of teaching developed at Harvard in the 1870s, gave students the vocational training they needed to practice the law but left them with a view of the law as a "dry, arid logic, divorced from society and life."[14]

The narrow, technical training of most nineteenth-century lawyers contributed to the lack of theoretical or conceptual thinking within the law. Even at the end of the nineteenth century, when the "scientific" approach of Christopher Columbus Langdell of the Harvard Law School emerged as the leading method of legal instruction, it was a teaching method designed to teach the absolute truths of legal science, not a model intended to help the student or practitioner understand the law or discover new ways of thinking about the law.[15]

The black letter approach to the law influenced freedom of the press case law. Its influence is most noticeable in the second half of the nineteenth century. Newspaper publishers attempted to establish special protection for the watchdog role of the press, but the claim was not a theoretically or conceptually based claim; it was just a response to the demands of the common law. Rather than developing a theory based on the watchdog concept, advocates of the watchdog role for the press merely asserted the claim and attempted to pile up supporting case law.

LEGAL SCHOLARSHIP

Judges produced the most important legal literature of the nineteenth century. Until the last decade of the century, lawyers relied on two printed sources for definitive interpretation of the law: printed case reports and legal treatises. Several law reviews were published earlier in the century, but the first edition of the *Harvard Law Review*, published in 1887, was the first modern law review. Earlier law reviews consisted of edited summaries of judicial opinions and treatiselike articles that did little more than recite the pertinent recent case law on a given subject.[16]

Judges' self-defined task in the nineteenth century was to announce the law, not to make law. This "oracular theory" of the role of a judge was based on a belief that the law was "a mystical body of permanent truths, and the judge was seen as one who declared what those truths were and made them intelligible."[17] The oracular theory did not survive the nineteenth century; however, the legal literature of the 1800s reflected this view of the judicial role and the nature of law. Judicial opinions, with rare exceptions, asserted the law with little discussion of underlying principles. In freedom-of-the-press case law, judges frequently praised the value of liberty of the press in a democracy while bemoaning the abuse of that liberty, but few judges go beyond assertions of the limits of freedom of the press and attempt to explain the reasons for those limits.

Before the Civil War, legal treatises were the only source of current law for lawyers working in isolated parts of the United States, and later in the century treatises provided an easy way for attorneys to find a path through the maze of late nineteenth-century common law. By the 1850s every state in the Union published reports of its highest appellate court decisions and by 1885 there were about 3,798 volumes of published reports. The establishment of the National Reporter System in 1879 and the beginning of the West Publishing Company's legal digests helped bring some order to the reporting of the common law, but no attorney could stay abreast of all the cases reported in the United States.[18] Legal treatises provided the practicing attorney with summaries and discussions of current case law and became the primary source of law. The treatment of the law in most treatises mirrored the pragmatic, narrow, technical approach to the law found in judicial opinions and legal education. However, although treatise writers did not explicitly discuss the social and political implications of the law, their selection and treatment of case law reflected the writers' views of public policy and the role of law in shaping society.

The treatises of Joseph Story and Thomas Cooley were

major influences on the definition of freedom of the press in the
1800s. Story has been called "the American Blackstone."[19] His
Commentaries became "a sufficient surrogate for the law itself
. . . the authorit[y] became authoritative."[20] Judges continually
cited Story as the authority in support of the common-law interpretation of freedom of the press.

Story attempted, in his writing both on the bench and in his
treatises, to create a body of American law. In the early 1800s,
judges did not have extensive law libraries. With the exception
of Tucker's edition of Blackstone, all the major published legal
treatises were English. Story worked to establish a body of
American legal writing with judge-made common law as its
foundation and provided the judiciary with the tools to protect
society from disorder and anarchy.[21]

His statement of the freedom of the press was cited
throughout the nineteenth century and well into the twentieth
century.

> That [freedom of the press] was intended to secure to every
> citizen an absolute right to speak, or write, or print what-
> ever he might please, without any responsibility, public or
> private . . . is a supposition too wild to be indulged by any
> rational man. This would allow to every citizen a right to
> destroy at his pleasure the reputation, the peace, the prop-
> erty, and even the personal safety of every other citizen.
> . . . It is plain then, that the language of [the First Amend-
> ment] imports no more than that every man shall have a
> right to speak, write, and print his opinions upon any sub-
> ject whatsoever, without prior restraint, so always that he
> does not injure any other person in his rights, person,
> property, or reputation; and so always that he does not
> thereby disturb the public peace, or attempt to subvert the
> government.[22]

He then noted that constitutional freedom of the press "is
neither more nor less than an expansion of the great doctrine
recently brought into operation in the law of libel, that every
man shall be at liberty to publish what is true, with good mo-

tives and for justifiable ends."[23] Having grounded the definition of constitutional freedom of the press in the common law, Story devoted almost ten pages to a defense of his interpretation. He summed up his defense in two sentences:

> The doctrine laid down by Mr. Justice Blackstone respecting the liberty of the press has not been repudiated, as far as is known, by any solemn decision of any State courts, in respect to their own municipal jurisprudence. On the contrary, it has been repeatedly affirmed in several of the States, not withstanding their constitutions or laws recognizing that "the liberty of the press ought not to be restrained," or more emphatically, that "the liberty of the press shall be inviolably maintained."[24]

Story is quoted at length because his Blackstonian definition of freedom of the press — not the words of the founding fathers or the drafters of state constitutional free-press clauses — was the most frequently cited authority in free-press case law prior to the publication of Cooley's *Constitutional Limitations*.[25] Also, Story's treatment of freedom of the press is representative of treatise writing in the 1800s. He stated his definition of the law and then recited a version of the history of English suppression of the press and legal authority to support his assertion. Story's treatment of the law, like most nineteenth-century treatises, lacked any discussion of the political or social philosophies underlying the black letter of the law.

By the second half of the nineteenth century a large body of American law and legal literature existed, but Cooley's *Constitutional Limitations* stands out as one of the most important legal works of the late 1800s. Cooley attempted, in this and his other legal writing, to adapt the law to the changing industrialized society of the time.[26]

Cooley and other judges in the late nineteenth century faced a challenge of preserving the continuity of the common law but at the same time changing the law to fit the demands of a rapidly changing world. Cooley's discussion of freedom of the press also reflected his attempt to reconcile the common law of Justice Story with the demands of an industrialized society and the public interest in the dissemination of information in a democracy.

Cooley's definition of the constitutional right to freedom of the press did not "assume to create new rights," but only to protect an existing common law right.

> The constitutional liberty of the press, as we understand it, implies a right to freely utter and publish whatever the citizen may please, and to be protected against any responsibility for so doing, except so far as such publications, from their blasphemy, obscenity, or scandalous character, may be a public offense, or as by their falsehood and malice they may injuriously affect the standing, reputation, or pecuniary interests of individuals.[27]

This definition is in agreement with Justice Story's. Had Cooley stopped at this point, he would have added little to Story's brief discussion of freedom of the press. But Cooley continued for nearly fifty pages in which he detailed the existing common law privileges in libel that "for some reason of general public policy" protected publication of certain types of false defamatory statements.[28]

Cooley found his interpretation of constitutional guarantees of freedom of the press in libel common-law privileges and the public's interest in "such free and general discussion of public matters as seems absolutely essential to prepare the people for an intelligent exercise of their rights as citizens."[29] Cooley suggested that the conditions of constitutional democracy in the United States required greater protection of freedom of the press than the protection granted under English common law, but his view of freedom of the press was a common-law conception adapted to fit the needs of American society in the late 1800s.

Cooley recognized the newspaper as being an important component in modern society. Newspapers, he said, had a pow-

erful influence on society because they provided the information
the public needed. While Cooley discussed the problems of
newspaper publishers under libel law, he concluded that relief
would not come from the common law. "Publishers," he wrote,
"must appeal to the protection of public opinion, or they must
call upon the legislature for such modification of the law as may
seem important to their just protection."[30]

The uncertainty in Cooley's discussion of freedom of the
press—on one hand he endorsed Story's Blackstonian view of
constitutional freedom, but on the other he wrote at some
length of the need for greater freedom of the press in a democracy—meant that Cooley was cited in court opinions attempting
to expand the limits of protected expression and in opinions
maintaining Story's limited conception of protected speech. But
regardless of the authority cited, the basis for determining the
limits of freedom of the press in the nineteenth century was
judicial perception of the public good as defined by majoritarian values.

PROTECTING THE MAJORITY

At the turn of the twentieth century, Associate Justice of
the United States Henry B. Brown told members of the New
York State Bar Association that "many [newspapers] are guilty
of a grave abuse of their privileges . . . much of the daily press
is lacking in good taste, the high moral tone and the general
fairness that should characterize those who aspire to be considered leaders of public opinion."[31] The law protected some of the
publications the justice criticized, but throughout the nineteenth
century judges deemed many publications to be beyond accept-
able limits of taste, morality, fairness, civility, or temper. No
contradiction existed in the minds of judges who wrote at some
length about the value of freedom of the press and then found
an unintentional libel, intemperate criticism, or crime news to be
an example of the licentiousness, not the liberty, of the press.

The use of the law to protect majoritarian interests at the expense of individual rights was not limited to freedom of the press. John Roche, in his study of civil liberties in the United States, found that "the whole notion of individual rights *enforceable against the community* . . . is a twentieth century legal innovation." While admitting that his survey of nineteenth-century case law might have overlooked isolated cases, Roche asserted that he had "yet to find an early case in which a state appellate court reversed a conviction below on the basis of a state bill of rights."[32]

Nineteenth-century judges viewed the law as an instrument for the protection and the improvement of society. Speech that did not contribute to the betterment of society or that disrupted the social order had no value, and therefore deserved no legal protection. For example, a Missouri court rejected a defendant's claim of freedom of the press and upheld a conviction under a statute that made it illegal to publish or sell newspapers "devoted mainly to the publication of scandal and immoral conduct." The court endorsed the legislature's attempt to stop such "corrupting and depraving influence[s]" from reaching the public.[33]

The judicial view of the proper limits of freedom of the press did not stop individuals from speaking out or stop publishers from printing newspapers. The press in the nineteenth century was vigorous and full of material that exceeded judicial standards of propriety. Clearly, the public's view of the limits of protected speech did not always agree with the law. The content and tone of the nineteenth-century press indicate the strong and widely held popular support for a citizen's right to criticize government officials. But the focus of this study is the legal definition of freedom of the press. Within the law, judges' instrumental view of the common law and the application of majoritarian standards established a limited and highly arbitrary protection for the freedom of the press.

For students of twentieth-century press law, discussion of the nineteenth-century common-law concept of freedom of the press requires different thinking about freedom of the press. The "preferred freedom" status of freedom of the press, which requires judges to examine with "more exacting judicial scrutiny" laws that restrain speech or press, is a twentieth-century view of the constitutional limitations placed on government's power to regulate the press in the public interest.[34]

Nineteenth-century judges and advocates shaped freedom of the press to meet the demands of the common law and majoritarian values. The common law of libel provided little protection for the publication of defamatory statements. Freedom of the press was a question of intent, justification, and the public interest. There were, for nineteenth-century jurists, many unprotected false ideas under the common law.[35] In this climate, newspaper publishers attempted to create special protections for the institutional press by incorporating the watchdog concept of freedom of the press into the common law.

4

The Watchdog in Nineteenth-Century Libel Law

HE common law of libel placed severe limits on the freedom of the press. In response to the demands of the common law, newspaper publishers attempted to establish the watchdog concept of freedom of the press that would protect the publication of otherwise unprotected defamatory material.

A judge in a Massachusetts courtroom in the late 1820s observed that "[w]henever there is an attempt to maintain a prosecution for libel, it almost necessarily brings under discussion the freedom of the press."[1] In the nineteenth century, debate over the meaning of freedom of the press took place in civil and criminal libel litigation, but the majority of litigation concerned civil libel actions.[2] Publishers adopted the status of institutional watchdogs serving the public interest throughout the century. With increasing frequency in the second half of the century, publishers fighting libel actions defined the press as being a distinct entity with a duty to the public to observe, investigate, and report public proceedings, the actions of public officials, and other matters of public interest. Newspaper advocates argued that the watchdog role required the creation of special protections in libel law for the press. Advocates at-

tempted to expand the common law of libel in order to carve out
a special niche for the press in the existing common-law privileges available to all citizens.

Common-law privilege was a means of operationalizing
freedom of the press. In contrast to the present, when freedom
of the press in libel law is seen primarily as a constitutional
question, the nineteenth- and early twentieth-century common
law defined the boundaries and meaning of freedom of the
press.[3]

The narrow privileges provided in the common law for
criticism of public officials and government and reporting on
judicial and legislative proceedings were crucibles in which
judges and advocates in libel suits struggled to preserve or to
reshape the common law and to interpret legislative efforts to
codify common-law privileges in statutes.[4] Much of the debate
concerned differing views of the public value of defamatory
publications and the role of newspapers in society. Advocates
for newspaper publishers urged the courts to establish the press
as an institutional watchdog by creating a more liberal privilege
for the watchdogs. However, judges throughout the nineteenth
century decried the policies and practices of a licentious press
and consistently found its reporting of libelous information to
be outside the bounds of privileged communication.[5]

As the commercial newspaper industry experienced rapid
growth after the Civil War and the newsgathering function grew
more complex and institutionalized, defendants described the
press as "public journals"[6] with a duty and responsibility to act
as a watchdog for the public in matters of government and
public importance. This use of the watchdog role of the press fit
very comfortably into a standard common-law analysis of conditional privilege. If the defendant in a civil libel suit could show
a duty or responsibility to report defamatory information because it served the public's interest, then the defendant could
win the suit or at least limit the damage award to the plaintiff.

Publishers' lack of success in creating a special niche for the
newspaper industry through the use of a watchdog concept of

freedom of the press does not diminish the significance of the effort. Nineteenth-century common-law libel is the first instance of a consistent and persistent use of the institutional watchdog concept in the history of freedom of the press in the United States. Identifying the common law and litigation as the primary influences on the development of the institutional watchdog concept of freedom of the press demonstrates the importance of these factors to the understanding of the development of freedom of the press in the United States.

The watchdog concept as it developed in nineteenth-century libel law was a creature of the common law. Newspaper publishers attempted to fashion a rationale for expanding the protection provided for freedom of the press under the common-law privilege by establishing in libel law an institutional role for the press as a servant of the public interest. This chapter briefly outlines privilege in the law of libel and traces the use and development of the watchdog metaphor in the forum of libel litigation.

COMMON LAW PRIVILEGE

The common law of libel protects certain types of communication from libel actions. The law limits a speaker's liability if he is sued for libel on the basis of defamatory statements contained in certain categories of communication. These categories are called privileged communications.

There are two general categories of privilege: absolute privilege, which prevents any civil libel action based on any statement made in specified forums; and conditional privilege, which provides some protection from liability if the speaker meets the requirements of the particular privilege. Meetings of a legislative body and judicial proceedings are two examples of forums in which speakers have an absolute privilege.[7]

Conditional privileges exist when the speaker has a duty or interest to communicate potentially libelous information to an audience that has a need or duty to receive the communication. For example, a conditional privilege exists in the following situations as long as the speaker is acting in good faith and without ill will: (1) when the victim of a robbery reports the name of a suspected thief to the police, (2) when a former employer is asked to write a letter of recommendation in connection with a job application, (3) in the dissemination of commercial credit information to subscribers to a credit bureau, and (4) in a letter to a public official requesting assistance with a matter of public concern.[8] In each of the above examples the relation of the duty to speak to the need to know the information is clear. In general terms, each of these privileges exists because the public interest is better served by protecting the communication than by permitting a defamed person to bring action to protect his or her reputation.

Three categories of conditional privilege are of primary concern to newspaper publishers: (1) fair report privilege—the right to publish a full and accurate report of public proceedings; (2) good faith misstatement of fact in communications to the public about matters of vital public interest; and (3) the privilege of fair comment—it protects the publication of defamatory opinion.[9] The good faith misstatement of fact privilege was not recognized in the nineteenth century. The extremely narrow definition of "opinion" under fair comment limited its value to newspaper publishers. Establishing a privilege to allow good faith mistakes in reports about matters of public concern was an important goal in the effort to establish the watchdog concept.

Privileges exist in the common law to protect the public interest in receiving certain types of information. They are intended to protect the individual's right to freedom of the press. Cooley explained the reason for protecting defamatory publications as follows:

> A question of defamation is therefore not always a question merely of private scandal; it may on the other hand, involve questions of the highest public importance. . . .
> We unhesitatingly recognize the fact that in many cases,

however damaging it may be to individuals [reputations], there should and must be legal immunity for free speaking, and that justice and the cause of good government would suffer if it were otherwise.[10]

In the nineteenth century, conditional privilege provided a defendant with a limited defense. It did not remove all liability but it shifted the burden of proving the existence of malice (that is, evidence that the libelous publication was the product of ill will or malicious intent) to the plaintiff. In a minority of jurisdictions later in the century, conditional privilege also removed the threat of punitive damages, but in the majority of jurisdictions the value of a conditional privilege to a defendant remained the same. "It properly signifies this and nothing more: that the excepted instances shall so far change the ordinary rule . . . as to remove the regular and usual presumption of malice, and make it incumbent on the party complaining to show malice."[11]

English courts first recognized a fair report privilege in 1795. In *Curry v. Walter*, a court held that a good faith report of judicial proceedings was not actionable provided the defendant proved the report to be "precisely the substance" of the proceeding. Four years later in *King v. Wright*, the court explained the rationale for protecting the publication of defamatory information gathered in court proceedings: "They are printed for the information of the public . . . Though the publication of such proceedings may be to the disadvantage of the particular individual concerned, yet it is of vast importance to the public that the proceedings of Courts of Justice should be universally known."[12]

The English courts limited the scope of the conditional privilege to court proceedings and conditioned the privilege on the accuracy of the report, the lack of any editorial comment, and the absence of ill will.[13]

A privilege protecting good faith misstatement of fact about matters of public concern was not recognized until 1908. In *Coleman v. MacLennan* the Kansas Supreme Court accepted the claim that the public interest in free and open discussion of public matters outweighed the protection of individual reputation.[14] This claim had been made in American courts as early as 1808, when counsel for one William Clap, who was on trial for criminal libel for posting a handbill calling a state-appointed auctioneer "a liar, a scoundrel, a cheat, and a swindler," argued for greater protection for such speech.

> [The] community have an interest in his integrity, and have a right to be informed what his conduct in office is, that they may judge whether it is safe and discreet to intrust their property to his care and management. . . . It is of much greater importance that this high constitutional privilege be preserved unimpaired, than that a libeller should now and then go unpunished.

The Massachusetts Supreme Judicial Court held that the public interest in public order and in protecting reputation were of greater importance than libelous publication about public officials. The balance struck in 1808 remained basically unchanged until the twentieth century.[15]

Conditional privileges developed as a means of ensuring that the needs of society as a whole were being served. In contrast to individualistic notions of freedom of the press familiar to students of twentieth-century constitutional law, a societal view of freedom of the press found in the common law shaped nineteenth-century thinking about the legal limits of freedom of expression. Privilege existed to protect the public interest in receiving certain kinds of information, not to protect the right of speakers to speak.[16]

In that the public interest was the paramount concern, the motive of the speaker was a determinative factor. If a speaker defamed another person with the intent of harming the individual rather than serving the public interest, the privilege was lost. Standards of evidence for proving malicious intent created difficult problems for courts in cases concerning two individuals, and as the newsgathering process became more complex the problem of establishing reasonable and workable standards of evidence of malice in cases brought against newspapers created greater uncertainty in the law of libel.[17]

Within the framework of the existing conditional privilege of fair report and the desired privilege of good faith reports about public officials, newspaper publishers attempted to define a relationship between newspaper publishers, editors, and reporters and the public to expand the boundaries of conditional privilege and thereby expand the protections of freedom of the press. They claimed a *duty* to observe, investigate, comment, and report on official proceedings of government and on the performance and moral character of public officials and candidates in order to serve the public interest. They assumed, for the purposes of defending against libel actions, the role of institutional watchdogs in a democratic society.

THE WATCHDOG

The concept of an institutional watchdog found in libel is in agreement with the checking value theory of freedom of the press. As stated by Vincent Blasi, the checking value of freedom of the press is based on "the idea that free expression is valuable in part because of the function it performs in checking the abuse of official power." Writers in colonial and revolutionary America discussed freedom of the press in terms of its checking value, and at least one state constitution provided for the checking value of freedom of the press.[18]

The Declaration of Rights in the Pennsylvania Constitution provided that "the freedom of the press shall not be restrained" and "printing presses shall be free to every person who undertakes to examine the proceedings of the legislature or any part of government." But in one of the earliest recorded cases in which a state court interpreted the meaning of a state constitution's freedom of the press clauses, the Pennsylvania Supreme Court looked to the narrow common-law view of freedom of the press to determine the meaning of the constitutional language.[19]

Chief Justice Thomas McKean identified motive and public benefit as two factors that limited the legal boundaries of freedom of the press. He explicitly rested his interpretation of the text of the free-press clauses in the state constitution on English common law. Though the state constitution gave "every citizen the right of investigating the conduct of those who are entrusted with the public business," the court said the constitution merely stated the existing common law. "The true liberty of the press is amply secured by permitting every man to publish his opinion; but it is due to the peace and dignity of society to inquire into the motives of such publications, and to distinguish between those which are meant for the use and reformation, and with an eye solely to the public good, and those which are intended merely to delude and defame."[20]

The Pennsylvania Supreme Court's definition of freedom of the press highlights the limited protection from libel actions in the late 1700s. Freedom of the press only extended to good faith statements of opinion or good faith statements of facts that held up when subjected to a severe and narrow standard of truth. The existing narrow fair report privilege was a shallow and relatively unprotected harbor on a rocky coast for publishers of newspapers.[21]

Publishers wanted the freedom to make mistakes. This freedom could be attained in the common law if (1) courts expanded the scope of the fair report privilege to include more than judicial proceedings, (2) courts created a privilege to report on the affairs of public officials and candidates, (3) the common law no longer presumed malice in civil suits, and (4) the common law recognized and incorporated the newsgathering process into the determination of malice.

Newspaper advocates used the watchdog role of the press as part of their effort to bring the above changes into the common law. The attempt to shape a special conditional privilege for the institutional press greater than the common-law privileges available to every citizen required that the role of the press be distinguished from the duty of every citizen to act as a check on the potential abuse of governmental power. Incorporation of the press's role as a watchdog into common-law privilege enabled publishers to claim a duty to report defamatory information concerning public figures or officials. The presence of a duty to report provided a proper, nonmalicious motive for publishing otherwise actionable statements, and thereby, a rationale for expanding protection of freedom of the press.

Early Signs of the Watchdog

The watchdog concept appeared in the early 1800s. Though it was not a major factor in libel case law until the last thirty years of the nineteenth century, publishers began to use it at the beginning of the century. Jurors responded favorably when advocates linked the functions of the institutional press to the strong American tradition of freedom of the press, but judges refused to grant publishers special status under the common law or to expand the existing narrow fair report privilege. They expressed distrust of publishers' motives and disapproval of the journalism of the day. The personal attacks and counterattacks in the political press did not meet judicial standards of propriety and rational discussion. Judges wondered how a licentious press served the public interest.[22]

As early as 1805, a newspaper publisher argued his duty to the public justified publication of a libel. The New York *Evening Post* published a story charging the superintendent of a county poorhouse with denying admission to a poor, pregnant black woman on a cold, snowy November night. A libel suit against William Coleman, the publisher and editor of the *Evening Post*, followed the publication.[23]

At trial, defendant's counsel argued that the story was a fair report of police records, and that the defendant, as an editor of a "public paper," had a "duty to keep a watchful eye over [public officials] and to call the attention of the public to any of their acts, which in his opinion are neglectful or criminal." He urged the jury to recognize the defendant's role as a public watchdog. "If . . . Mr. Coleman has done no more . . . than exercise his right as an editor, and his duty to the public, it is impossible you should find a verdict against him."[24]

In other early nineteenth-century cases, lawyers told juries that "indulgence should be shown to . . . the conductors of a press, whose duty is to communicate to their readers what passes in the legislature." Newspapers served the public interest by, advocates said, "proclaim[ing] the vices and abuses of government."[25]

Although jurors responded favorably to defendants' claims of duty and public interest, the bench found little merit in the argument. State trial and appellate court judges repeatedly rejected publishers' claim of special protection for newspapers. In denying a motion for a new trial, the New York Supreme Court said "it is denied that . . . editors of a newspaper . . . have any other rights than such as are common to all."[26]

Newspapers continually overstepped the bounds of the fair report privilege, and as a result ended up exposed to libel actions. Privilege only protected a paper's report of official governmental proceedings. It did not protect reports based on official records, *ex parte* judicial proceedings, or the nonofficial actions of legislators relating to their official conduct. For example, a report that New York State's lieutenant governor was drunk while on the floor of the state legislature during an important proceeding fell outside the privilege.[27]

Publishers wanted judges to expand the privilege, but judges did not see the public value in allowing newspapers to publish libels against public men. Judges' opinions exhibited the bench's distrust of the press's ability or desire to serve the public interest in a responsible fashion if freed of legal constraints. One trial judge asked a jury, "Does the public taste demand these bitter and unmitigated aspersions of private reputation which so crowd the newspapers of the day?" His answer offered little hope to newspaper publishers. "[A] jury could render no more meritorious service to the public, than by repressing this enormous evil. It can be done only by visiting, with severe damages, him who wantonly and falsely assails the character of another through the public papers."[28]

Chief Judge Nelson of the Supreme Court of New York added his voice to the chorus of judicial critics of the press, noting that perhaps statutory relief for publishers should be granted, as the defendants had suggested, "if it be desirable to pamper a depraved public appetite or taste . . . by the re-publication of all the falsehoods and calumnies upon private character that may find their way into the press—to give encouragement to the widest possible circulation of these vile and defamatory publications, by protecting the retailers of them."[29]

Joseph Story's opinion in *Arnold v. Clifford*, a fair report case in a Rhode Island federal circuit court, represented the majority view on the bench. Justice Story said newspapers had a privilege to report judicial proceedings, but no right to publish testimony that libeled an individual. "There is no such right recognized in civil society, or at least in our forms of government, as the right of slandering or calumniating another. The liberty of the press does not include the right to publish libels."[30]

Story's rejection of a more liberal privilege paralleled his view of the limits of federal constitutional protection of freedom of the press. In *The Constitution of the United States*, Story dismissed claims of special protection for the press and other liberal free-press claims as nothing more than "loose reasoning on the subject of freedom of the press," which were "too extravagant to be held by any sound constitutional lawyer." He limited freedom of the press to Blackstone's common-law protections.[31]

Story's Blackstonian view of freedom of the press in both common law and constitutional contexts was the dominant position in state courts throughout the United States in the 1840s. Publishers claimed special protection for the watchdog press, but the words of a Boston Municipal Court trial judge's jury

instructions suggest the unfriendly reception given to the claim
in most courtrooms. "It has been argued by the defendant, that
there is in this commonwealth no law making a man punishable
for the publication of a libel in the public press. The court
instructs you, gentlemen, that there is no such doctrine." After
deliberating for fifteen minutes, the jury returned a guilty verdict against the publisher of the *Daily Chronotype*.[32]

The Commercial Press

The growth of a commercial newspaper industry in the
United States introduced new questions into the law of libel.
News was the primary product of the commercial newspaper
industry. As newspapers became large organizations with layers
of authority and responsibility, the increased complexity of the
newspaper editorial process complicated the legal issues present
in libel litigation. Publishers, editors, correspondents, and
"news-collectors" all had a hand in generating the news.[33]

Publishers argued that libel law should be changed to account for the "peculiarity of their profession" and the difficulty
of determining the truth. David Dudley Field, counsel for James
Gordon Bennett's New York *Herald*, argued that the standard of
proof for newspaper editors should not rest on "whether the
facts stated are true, but whether the [editor] believed them to
be true."[34] Field reasoned that demanding absolute knowledge
of truth from newspapers was too severe a standard given the
complexity of the newsgathering process.

In *Sheckell v. Jackson*, counsel for the publisher attempted
to introduce testimony from the news-collector detailing "what
inquiries and examinations he made, and what sources of information he applied to," and urged the court to instruct the jury
that the "public press are entitled to especial rights and privileges," because the defendant had a "duty to perform, and [if] in
the performance of that duty [he] states honestly what he be-

lieves to be true, the occasion furnishes a justification for the statement, though he may be mistaken." The trial judge told the jury that "the defendant's case does not come within the privileged or excepted cases."[35]

On appeal, the Supreme Judicial Court of Massachusetts affirmed the verdict for the plaintiff. Chief Justice Lemuel Shaw wrote that the press "have just the same rights as the rest of the community. They have the right to publish the truth, but no right to publish falsehoods to the injury of others with impunity."[36]

Crime news, a staple of the commercial press after the Civil War, was a fertile field for libel litigation from the 1850s to the end of the century. Though judges acknowledged the press's role as the "chronicler of events" and the "channels of communicating general and important information," the law declined to accept the claims of special protection put forward by publishers. Instead, the majority of judges shared the view of the Connecticut Supreme Court in *Moore v. Stevenson.*

> Newspapers are looked to as the channels of communicating general and important information; but even here we may demand from an editor, whether he be himself the author, or only opens his columns to others, that he exercise the care and vigilance of a prudent and conscientious man yielding the power of the public press. Nothing will be gained by too much relaxation of the law of libel.[37]

Courts refused to expand the limits of the fair report privilege, in part because of judges' displeasure with the increased sensational reporting of crime news and the insertion of editorial comment into crime and trial stories. In Louisiana, the publisher of the New Orleans *Crescent* lost a libel suit brought by a sea captain because its report of his arrest was "exaggerated and inflammatory" and "assured and proclaimed" the guilt of the captain. The Ohio Supreme Court affirmed a libel judgment against the publisher of the Hamilton *Telegraph* for reporting that a state official had been charged with illegally diverting state funds and observing that he "had become . . . notorious for depravity, recklessness, and peculation."[38]

The Watchdog Arrives: 1860–1890

After the Civil War, publishers increasingly turned to the watchdog. The use of the watchdog conception of freedom of the press in the late 1860s signaled the beginning of more than three decades during which publishers defended editorial and newsgathering practices in terms of their duty to serve the public interest. The watchdog function required, publishers argued, that they be shielded from libel actions brought by public officials, candidates for public office, and individuals caught in the criminal justice system.

A South Carolina lawyer's statement to a jury misstated the law as it existed but stated clearly the law publishers desired. "Considering the mission of the press in modern society it is not difficult to discover why it has been singled out as it has for special protection. It is because the comments of the free press are ofttimes the only protection against official corruption and venality."[39]

The number of litigated libel suits exploded after the Civil War. In case after case newspaper publishers argued for special privilege and asked judges and juries to consider the watchdog role of the press in modern society. In addition to litigation, the newspaper industry attempted to get protective legislation passed. Libel law was one of the first industry problems addressed by the American Newspaper Publishers Association (ANPA) and the National Editorial Association (NEA). In the late 1880s and early 1890s both groups were engaged in efforts to pass state and federal libel laws.[40]

The rise in the number of libel suits is explained, in part, by the rapid increase in the number of newspapers in the second half of the nineteenth century. The number of daily newspapers published in the United States rose from 254 in 1850 to 574 in 1870 and 971 in 1880.[41]

Moreover, the case law suggests that newspapers' proclivity toward convicting defendants in criminal actions and inserting editorial comment into news reports generated libel suits. Judges continued to tell publishers that sensational, intemperate, and false information did not serve the public good.

Two cases at the end of the 1860s illustrate the utility of the watchdog role of the press in fashioning a protection within libel law. When courts did accept the press's watchdog role, they fashioned greater protection in libel law for the newsgathering functions of the press. When courts rejected the watchdog claim, the common law of libel remained unchanged.

In *Smith v. Tribune*, a federal district court judge rejected a defendant's claim of special privilege to report about public officials.

> [I]t is not an answer to say that [Smith] is a public man . . . and that the defendants are the publishers of a newspaper . . . [Freedom of the press] has never been understood as authorizing the bringing of charges against a man . . . unless those charges were true . . . I hardly think that with an honest motive a journalist has a right to proclaim to the world that a particular man is a thief.[42]

But in *Detroit Daily Post v. McArthur*, the Michigan Supreme Court acknowledged the institutional role of the press. "A special protection for newspapers within the common law was necessary," Justice Cambell wrote, "inasmuch as the newspaper press is one of the necessities of civilization, the conditions under which it is required to be conducted should not be unreasonable or vexatious."[43]

Because the press served the public interest, the court addressed the questions raised by the institutional practices and constraints of the newspaper business. "There is no doubt," the court said, "of the duty of every publisher to see at all hazards that no libel appears in his paper." But if the publisher could prove he had employed competent editors, and had instituted rules and practices to prevent libels from appearing in his paper, the freedom of the press prevented the awarding of punitive damages.[44]

When judges accepted the watchdog concept, publishers received greater protection from libel suits, but most courts continued to reject the watchdog claims of publishers. The content and tone of the libels before the bench continued to contribute to judicial resistance of the watchdog concept.

A Sensational Press

The following selections from libel suits brought in the 1870s illustrate the type of reports that generated libel actions.

In a story reporting a guilty verdict, a Colorado paper judged the performance of the jury: "We cannot express the contempt which should be felt for these twelve men, who have thus not only offended public opinion, but have done an injustice to their own oaths."[45]

A Maryland newspaper reported an arrest and holding over for grand jury on a charge of indecent exposure. "THE RUFFIAN CAGED . . . It appears he is a low character who habitually frequents the streets and seeks to throw himself in the way of school girls."[46]

The *Pioneer Press* in Minnesota began an erroneous report of the arrest of a telegraph operator with the following lead: "The Pine City telegraph operator is a bad one. He is now under arrest for attempting to ravish a Swede woman."[47]

The Chicago *Times* published a false report of a coroner's inquest in which it reported that the widow of the subject of the inquest had a child by another man.[48]

Articles concerning elected officials and candidates also generated libel suits in the 1870s. During the political press period, politicians responded to harsh criticism and falsehood in the press. By the 1870s, political figures responded to false or questionable charges by filing libel suits. Stories that prompted these suits included one in a Kalamazoo, Michigan, paper reporting that a candidate for Congress on the Prohibition ticket was "convicted of stealing whiskey fines" and was a "pettifogging shyster" who had lost his position in a local church because he was an adulterer. Finally, a report in an Indiana paper stated that one candidate was "running for Congress not on any platform or well defined issue . . . but simply on beer and bribery."[49]

Judges stated their disapproval of the tone and content of the newspaper press. The criticism of the Chief Justice Lawrence of the Illinois Supreme Court reflects a commonly held view in the judiciary of the late 1800s.

> The article in question, grossly libelous as it is, is a kind lamentably frequent in the columns of American newspapers. There is probably no country in the civilized world where private character has so little security against newspaper assault. The conductors of the press . . . are singularly reckless in the exercise of their great power . . . [i]n pandering to the morbid taste of their readers for personal and worthless gossip.[50]

The state of the American press made it "difficult to see," Chief Justice Lawrence said, "how the public is to be benefited" by such reports or why the courts or legislatures should create protection for such a press.[51]

The Duty to Report the News

The watchdog concept of freedom of the press answered judicial criticism. The institutional press should be protected because it had a public duty to perform. The excesses of the press were regrettable, but the duty to gather the news in the public interest outweighed the harm caused by newspapers' transgressions.

An excerpt of a reporter's testimony in *Marks v. Baker* illustrates the value of the watchdog role as a defense. A candidate for city treasurer brought suit after a newspaper charged him with embezzling city funds.

Q: What was your object in publishing the article?

A: I published it for the general public interest.

Q: Did you have any other object in publishing the article?

A: I did not.

Q: You have stated that you had no other purpose than doing a public duty in publishing the article. I want to know what your object was—to charge someone with a crime, or whether you had some other object?

A: To draw attention to the discrepancy of the two reports. I had seen what purported to be the official report of the county auditor, and I had seen the city reporter's report.[52]

The duty to publish in the public interest established a proper motive and justification for defaming public officials. Judge Cooley wrote one of the clearest statements on the importance of the watchdog duty. "Few duties can be plainer than to challenge public attention to the official disregard of the principles which protect public and personal liberty."[53]

In Pennsylvania, the Supreme Court expanded the watchdog role of the press to include investigation of a privately owned "School for Clerks," stating that "the press was in the strict line of its duty when it sought to show that the plaintiff was a charlatan."[54]

But the courts' power to measure the public benefit of the watchdog's performance of its role made for uncertainty. In *Bourreseau v. Detroit Evening Journal Co.*, the Michigan Supreme Court rejected a claim of privilege for a story reporting that "justices and constables" of a Michigan township made a practice of "careless and unwarranted arrests" of persons passing through the area. The newspaper claimed privilege because "as a public journal, in pursuance of its duty, [it] felt compelled to lay before the public generally the statements gathered by its reporters." The Court disagreed saying that the publication of unproven charges did not serve the public good.[55]

The different standards applied in *Press Co.* and *Bourreseau* suggest the problem confronting publishers who were attempting to fashion a defense of conditional privilege to report about matters of public concern. Some courts had accepted the claim that the watchdog concept established an institutional duty, but judges disagreed over the protection the watchdog created. This uncertainty reduced the value of the privilege to publishers and diminished newspapers' ability to act as an institutional watchdog. As Justice Cooley observed in an 1881 dissent, "Who would venture to expose a swindler or a blackmailer . . . if every word and sentence must be uttered with judicial calmness and impartiality . . . and every fact and every inference be justified by unquestionable legal evidence?"[56]

For the watchdog to provide a meaningful defense, the complexity and uncertainty of newsgathering had to be taken into account, and duty rather than absolute accuracy had to become the dominant factor in determining the scope of the privilege. Publishers wanted to remove the burden of assumed malice.

Newsgathering

Michigan courts led the way in exploring the process of gathering news and its relation to proving malice. Whereas courts had previously held that the responsibility to publish the truth required papers to wait until they were absolutely certain of the truth of an article, the Michigan Supreme Court recognized the timeliness of news and reasoned that the "laudable desire on the part of publishers to give their readers the very latest and most reliable news" should be taken into account in determining malice. In order for a plaintiff to be awarded exemplary damages, the court said, the plaintiff had to prove negligence on the part of the defendant. The mere publication of a false defamatory statement did not constitute negligence; rather, the jury must consider "all the surrounding circumstances." If a publisher acted "with an earnest desire to give the public what he considered an important item of news, haste in so doing would be praiseworthy . . . and the time [the publisher] had for investigation and deliberation might well be considered in mitigation of damages."[57]

Efforts to take newsgathering into account for determining the proper standards of evidence for malice were directly linked to the court's view of the press as an institutional watchdog. Judge Cooley, concurring in *Foster v. Scripps*, a libel case brought by a physician employed by the city of Detroit, stated the basic rationale for privilege. "The reason for permitting a privilege of discussion in the case of a city physician must be this; that by operating on public opinion through the means of public discussion, the board having power of removal might indirectly be influenced, and a removal brought about in the case of an unfit officer."[58] One year later, when the same case returned to the Supreme Court on another point of law, Justice Marston identified the press's role, saying that "it would seem as though the public newspapers of the present day had not only the right, but that it was their duty to take part in the discussion of these matters which relate to the health, welfare, comfort and happiness of the people."[59] By the end of the decade, the Michigan court had created a conditional privilege limiting damages for "an honest mistake . . . made in an honest attempt to enlighten the public" about public officials or candidates for public office.[60]

The watchdog concept helped establish a limited privilege in Michigan, but it also gave judges an opportunity to evaluate the newsgathering practices in Michigan newspapers. A newspaper's duty, as defined by the court, "is to investigate the facts and endeavor to give the public accurate information."[61]

In 1889, the Michigan Supreme Court was provided the opportunity to examine the conduct of reporters and editors

when the Detroit *Free Press* published a report of the arrest of
two men in Windsor, Ontario, on a charge of illegally selling
postage stamps. At trial, the reporter who wrote the story was
questioned at length about the sources and the manner in which
he gathered the information for the report. Justice Morse took a
dim view of the reporter's performance.

> [T]he item . . . was printed as a matter of fact coming
> from Windsor, when in fact it was written by an employee
> of the paper at Detroit, entirely from hearsay. He could
> have personally investigated the matter, but did not do so.
> He did not ask to see the men . . . He did not talk to the
> postmaster . . . The only thing he saw with his own eyes —
> the complaint — he does not mention in his publication.
> . . . Nor was any care shown by the newspaper, it was, as
> far as the record shows, published as handed in by the
> reporter, without thought of verification.[62]

Having determined that the paper had not acted responsibly,
Justice Morse suggested something other than the public good
was behind the newspaper's claim of special protection.

> It is argued that a newspaper in this day and age of the
> world, when people are hungry for the news, and almost
> every person is a newspaper reader, must be allowed some
> latitude and more privilege than is ordinarily given under
> the law . . . In other words, because the world is thirsting
> for criminal items . . . there should be given greater im-
> munity to gossip in newspapers.

This "sophistry of reasoning," the judge said, did not provide a
rationale for giving the press any special protection from libel
actions.[63]

Other states echoed the Michigan court's recognition of the
relation between the watchdog concept and newsgathering. The
California Supreme Court limited publishers' liability for libels
published in the "usual course of the defendant's business as
public journalists," stating that "the public interest, and a due

regard for freedom of the press demands that its conductors should not be mulcted in punitive damages for publications on subjects of public interest, made for laudable motives, after due inquiry as to the truth of the facts stated, and in the honest belief that they were true."[64]

One of the strongest statements of the link between the role of the press as an institutional watchdog, the expansion of the press's privilege under libel law, and the basis of both the watchdog role and the expansion of protection in the public interest, is found in a report of a trial judge's instruction to a Pennsylvania Common Pleas Court jury.[65]

> The defendants are publishers of a public journal. It was their right, and perhaps their duty to call attention to and make comments upon the manner in which public buildings were being erected . . . The public is frequently slow and apathetic about matters of its own concern. It is not infrequently a little deaf, and the newspapers must halloo pretty loud to attract its attention.

But editors and reporters had a tendency, the judge continued, "to make a spicy paragraph at someone's expense. This is an abuse of the proper freedom of the press."[66]

A Missouri federal district court judge instructed the jury to take into account in determining damages the logistical and practical problems inherent in gathering news "because it is the function and duty of newspapers to furnish information to its readers of the current events. I say it would be a physical impossibility to send an agent to every place . . . to ascertain by personal examination the exact facts. A paper could not give us all which we have a right to hear of the current events of the day."[67]

And in Pennsylvania, the state supreme court held that "a public newspaper has a right to make inquiries regarding the official conduct of a public officer, and to publish reasonable comment and fair criticism upon it." If the paper used "ordinary care, such as is proper under the circumstances to ascertain the facts" in gathering the information, the publication was privileged.[68]

However, the success of the watchdog concept was limited. Most jurisdictions did not accept the publishers' claim. In Maryland, the publisher of the Hagerstown *Herald and Torchlight* claimed privilege for a story accusing a state senator of bribery and fraudulent activity in connection with a printing contract. The senator's actions, he argued, were "proper subjects for investigation and information" and the size and population of the county mandated the paper's publication of the information in the public interest. Judge Crompton dismissed the publisher's watchdog claim: "I am at a loss to see how anyone has a right to go beyond fair comment or discussion and impute base motives merely because he believes them to be true . . . The fact that one is a proprietor of a newspaper entitles him to no privilege . . . not possessed by the community in general."[69]

The gradual and uneven expansion of the right of editors and publishers to make good faith errors in reporting matters of public importance was the result of what the fourth edition of Townshend's *A Treatise on the Wrongs Called Libel and Slander* described as an "argu[ment] that the exigencies of the business of a newspaper editor, demand a larger amount of freedom." The gains of the publishers in a few states were significant but fell far short of the desired protection. In most jurisdictions, the effort failed. Townshend stated that "the law takes no judicial cognizance of newspapers . . . [and] recognizes no distinction in principle between the publication by the proprietor of a newspaper and a publication by any other individual."[70]

In 1879, the New Hampshire Supreme Court provided a terse statement of the status of the institutional role of the press under the law of libel. The defendants "make a loose averment to their general duty to give the readers such news as they might properly judge to be of interest and value to the community . . . They laid stress upon their business of publishing a newspaper. But professional publishers of news are not exempt, as a privileged class."[71]

After two decades of frequent attempts to expand privilege through the use of the watchdog concept, the case reports show little success. Michigan and a few other states had recognized the problems in the newsgathering process, but the general rule remained the same: "The publisher or proprietor of a newspaper stands before the court and before a jury like any other man . . . if there is any class in a community who ought to be careful that no harm is done, it is the proprietors who are in charge of this powerful engine—the press."[72]

Even though some courts were recognizing the newsgathering problems of the press, a Kentucky Court of Appeals ruling in 1889 presented the majority attitude, arguing that "it is said that it would be a harsh rule to require conductors of newspapers to be responsible for the truth of the information that they furnish to the public. . . . If it is not known to be true, do not publish it.[73]"

The Watchdog at the End of the Century

However, newspapers continued to claim special privilege based on their adopted role as institutional watchdog and the need for special protection for the newsgathering function. The testimony of an editor in *Edwards v. San Jose Printing & Publishing Co.* suggests that the notion of the press as an institutional watchdog had become part of editors' and reporters' view of the profession. When questioned about the publication of a charge of vote buying against an executive of an electric power company, the editor presented his role as a public watchdog as his justification for publishing the report. "I used the license and liberty which I had, as editor of the paper, to announce the [vote buying] . . . and I did it for the purpose of warning the company against anything of that kind . . . I did it for a good purpose and to prevent the very thing which it was feared would occur." But the California Supreme Court rejected the justification stating that "the mere belief of the editor of a newspaper in the justice and truth of an attack . . . is no defense."[74]

A Missouri Court of Appeals refused to accept a publisher's claim that a false report identifying a Mr. Arnold as the person who had stolen money from a local hospital was privileged because it was a report of police business and the result of "a common newspaper mistake."[75]

In *Ex parte Barry*, the California Supreme Court drew a narrow line between the watchdog's duty "to expose and bring to light any wrongful, corrupt, or improper act of a judicial officer" and the licentiousness of the press. "The great trouble with the freedom of the press at the present day, so far as it affects the courts," it said, "is that it is used indiscriminately . . . to gratify ill will and passion, or to pander to the passions or prejudices of others."[76] The court acknowledged the watchdog role of the press, but kept the dog on a very short leash.

The supreme court of Louisiana delivered a similar message to the press in *Fitzpatrick v. Daily States Publishing*. Counsel for the publishing company claimed "that it is the duty of an American Newspaper to keep the public advised of all matters of general interest; and to aid in securing good and faithful government." At trial the managing editor testified that "he regarded 'a newspaper as the notary of the people, and, when there is any act of corruption among any public officers [he] considers it the duty of the newspaper to take notice of it' . . . and he 'thought [he] would be recreant to [his] duty as a public journalist if [he] did not expose what [he] thought to be rascality.' "[77]

The court agreed that the press was a watchdog, but it found an editorial titled "A Den of Thieves," in which the newspaper called the mayor and other members of city government "blackmailers and bribe takers" and accused them of fraud and taking kickbacks, to be beyond the limits of freedom of the press. The watchdog role, the court said, "can be accomplished through the instrumentality of cogent, temperate, and well reasoned editorials . . . This rule . . . will greatly tend to the promotion of truth, good morals, and good citizenship."[78]

But in *Upton v. Hume* the Oregon Supreme Court reversed a judgment for a congressional candidate whom the *Gold Beach Gazette* had editorialized as a "loathsome, venomous thing without shame . . . an infamous scoundrel; and a perjured villain . . . The men who voted for the old forger Upton were thieves, robbers and sons of bitches." The court held that the editorial was privileged because of the "duty of the public press to discuss candidates."[79]

The Oregon court held a minority view of the protection in libel law for the press's watchdog role. The majority of courts continued to acknowledge the institutional role of the press, but to limit the protection provided by that role. The general concern of judges and their view of the press was summed up by Judge Stiness of the Rhode Island Supreme Court when he said that "as a publisher of news and items of public importance the press should have the freest scope, but as a scandal monger it should be held to the most rigid limitation."[80]

The majority of courts continued to examine the intent of the publisher and the justification for publications in determining the protection provided by freedom of the press. Publishers had convinced the courts that they had a public duty to observe and report on matters of public concern, but they had failed in the attempt to establish special protections for the news-gathering and publishing aspects of the newspaper industry. As the nineteenth century closed, the press had positioned itself in the common law as a watchdog serving the public interest, but the majority of courts continued to distrust the watchdog.

During the nineteenth century, common-law privilege provided only limited "breathing space" for newspaper publishers, editors, and reporters. The fair report privilege was narrowly interpreted and a privilege protecting good faith misstatements of facts in reports about matters of public concern had yet to be recognized.[81] And the existing common-law privileges did not provide adequate protection for the news content of late nineteenth-century newspapers. For example, reports of crime news and allegations of malfeasance on the part of public officials fell outside common-law privileges. Therefore, as newsgathering and the reporting of factual information became a primary function of the commercial press, publishers faced a growing number of libel actions in which they had the difficult task of proving their good intentions and justifying the publication of false information.

One response to this legal problem was an increased use of the watchdog concept as an argument for greater protections for the institutional press. American courts had liberalized the English common-law privileges in recognition of the need for an informed public in a constitutional representative democracy. The watchdog concept piggybacked the institutional press onto the established liberal concept of a watchdog public. In the language of common-law privilege, the need for an informed public created a duty to discuss matters of public concern. The institutional press, publishers argued, had a duty to provide the watchdog public with information; therefore, the institutional press required special protections under freedom of the press.

The watchdog concept, as defined by advocates for the newspaper industry, created a duty on the part of a newspaper publisher to serve the needs of the public. Because a publisher had a duty to serve the public interest, and the publication of information about the actions of government served that interest, he acted without malice, and therefore, the publication should be privileged.

The history of publishers' use of the watchdog concept of freedom of the press in nineteenth-century libel law shows the influence of the common law, the practice of law, and the adversarial process on the development of the meaning of freedom of the press. Newspaper publishers were confronted with a specific legal problem and they fashioned a response to that problem. Libel case law in the nineteenth century is full of assertions that publishers, editors, and reporters are protected by freedom of the press, but it is devoid of attempts to explain or understand the meaning of that freedom. In nineteenth-century libel law, the language of free-press advocates was the language of nineteenth-century common law. Within that common law, the institutional press attempted to fashion a legal protection that would shield the newsgathering and reporting practices of the industry. The result was the watchdog concept of freedom of the press.

CHAPTER

5

Contempt by Publication:
Where Was the Watchdog?

I N sharp contrast to newspaper publishers' use of the
watchdog in libel law, the watchdog concept was not an
important factor in nineteenth-century contempt case law.
Newspaper litigants in nineteenth-century libel litigation
positioned the press as a servant of the public interest in order to
establish an advantage within the legal constraint of common-
law libel. However, advocates placed little emphasis on the
watchdog concept in nineteenth-century contempt cases involving comment, criticism, and reporting about the judicial branch
of government. The contrast between the use of the watchdog
concept in libel and in contempt demonstrates the importance of
the common law of libel to the development of the watchdog
concept.

In the nineteenth century most of the contempt actions
brought against newspaper publishers, editors, and reporters
were for contempt by publication. Using common-law summary
contempt power, judges fined or jailed journalists for news reports or editorials concerning the activities of judges or ongoing
judicial proceedings. In all of the contempt cases reviewed, the
nature of the activity for which the reporter or publication faced
punishment could be characterized as part of the watchdog

function of the press: reporters and editors gathering and commenting upon information about the activities of government for the benefit of the public.

Judicial use of the contempt power to punish for the publication of facts, comment, or criticism of a judge or court highlights a central conflict in American constitutional democracy: on one hand, autocratic use of power by the judiciary and on the other hand the strongly held republican right of the people to freely discuss and criticize the government.[1] The balance between these two interests shifted during the 1800s. As a result, the use of contempt power to punish the press increased after the end of the Civil War.

In the first half of the nineteenth century a widely held distrust of judges and lawyers checked judges' use of contempt power. For example, a judge in New York thought a publication was a "most foolish, intemperate and unjustifiable production, written merely to gratify personal resentment," but did not exercise his contempt power.[2] As a result, a publisher could successfully defend against a contempt by wrapping himself in the public's right to freedom of the press, portraying the judge as an autocratic abuser of judicial power. But beginning in the late 1860s and with increasing frequency during the last three decades of the century, judges used summary contempt powers against the press.

In addition to the general reluctance to use the contempt power, the watchdog role of the press did not fit into the common law of contempt. Under the common law, a judge's power to hold an individual in constructive contempt required a finding of intent to influence a pending judicial proceeding. If a newspaper publisher had argued, as few did, that he had an institutional duty to act as a watchdog over the courts, the court could easily conclude that he intended to influence the proceedings of the court. Though judges readily agreed that the people had the right to criticize the performance of the legal system, they jealously guarded their right to keep the press's influence out of the courtroom.

Beginning in the late 1860s, the checks on judges' use of the contempt power eroded and the number of reported contempt cases increased. The watchdog role of the press was present in the case law, but its presence was minor and had little impact on the law of contempt or the results in contempt by publication litigation.

The following discussion outlines the law of contempt and traces the use of the contempt power against newspaper interests. Highlighting the lack of the watchdog role of the press in this area of law illustrates that the watchdog concept was a response to the requirements of common-law libel.

CONTEMPT BY PUBLICATION

A judge's power to hold a journalist in contempt for publishing material concerning ongoing judicial proceedings without an indictment and trial by jury clearly existed in nineteenth-century English and American common law, but its origins are suspect. Prior to Blackstone's era, no such power existed. Legal historians agree that no sound basis existed for Blackstone's assertion that "the method, immemorially used by the superior courts of justice, of punishing contempts by attachment" included the power to punish "speaking or writing contemptuously of the court or judges acting in their judicial capacity." Blackstone based his claim on an undelivered opinion in *The King v. Almon* written by Mr. Justice Wilmot, lord chief justice of the Court of Common Pleas and a personal friend of Blackstone.[3]

Sir John Fox established the questionable origins of contempt by publication in *History of Contempt of Court*, published in 1927, but the issue had been raised in the nineteenth century. One writer in the *American Law Register* noted that "[f]or any clearly ascertained and definite source of this power in the common law, or any decision or enactment giving rise to it . . . we may look in vain."[4]

However questionable its origins, courts had the power to summarily punish contempts by publication. Stewart Rapalje, in *A Treatise On Contempt*, recognized as the first American treatise on the subject, defined contempt by publication, stating that "any publication, pending a suit, reflecting on the court, the parties to the suit, the witnesses, the jurors or the counsel, is a contempt of court." In order for a publication to be a contempt, it had to refer to an ongoing or pending proceeding. It was assumed that publications concerning ongoing litigation would, Rapalje said, "have a tendency to prejudice the public with respect to merits of a cause depending in court, and to corrupt the administration of justice."[5]

The combination in the common law of a bad tendency doctrine and the summary power of a sitting judge posed a serious threat to those who wished to criticize the courts. But the American tradition of freedom of the press and legislative restraints checked judicial use of contempt power before the Civil War.

The tradition of freedom of the press as a component of republican liberty was the strongest check on abuse of the contempt power. Judges hesitated before using contempt power against newspapers. Rapalje observed that the "force of public opinion in this country, in favor of freedom of the press, has restrained the free exercise of the power to punish this class of contempts."[6]

Another factor—the threat of the power of the press—also may have played a part in limiting judges' use of contempt by publication. Many state court judges were elected and needed the support of the newspapers. In 1888, Samuel Merrill, an attorney employed by the Boston *Globe*, articulated both the public distrust of judicial power and the danger to an elected judge who was perceived to have abused his power.

> On account of its arbitrary character, the power of the courts in matters of contempt has always been looked upon with great jealousy in the United States. . . . The

newspaper has become such an important factor in business and society, that its interests are identified with those of the public; and the interests of neither the press nor the people at large are subserved by the summary punishment of an editor or newspaper writer for the publication of facts or opinions which happen to be distasteful to a judge.[7]

Pennsylvania passed the first statute limiting judges' summary contempt power. The law confined judges' summary contempt power to punishment of direct contempts and explicitly removed judicial power of contempt by publication. By the end of the century, thirty-four of the forty-five states had such statutes. By 1831, Congress passed a law removing the power of constructive contempt from the federal judiciary.[8]

Legislative limits worked to some degree, but many state courts strangled contempt statutes. Using legal sleight of hand, judges narrowly interpreted the statutes, and at the same time asserted the inherent power of the court to preserve and protect itself through the use of summary contempt powers. In the second half of the century, courts in seventeen states reasserted judicial power to punish contempt by publication.[9]

By the end of the nineteenth century, the use of constructive contempt against newspapers increased dramatically. The watchdog role of the press appeared but it had little visible impact on judicial wielding of contempt power against newspapers.

THE WATCHDOG IN CONTEMPT BY PUBLICATION

The watchdog concept first appeared in *Stuart v. People*, an 1842 contempt by publication against an editor of the Chicago *American*.[10] However, judges established the rationales for using judicial power to hold newspaper publishers and editors in contempt for publication in the early 1800s. Examination of the major themes presented in these earlier cases provides context for understanding the minimal use and the ineffectiveness of the watchdog concept in contempt cases.

The heart of contempt by publication is an assumption of the prejudicial influence of publicity about ongoing judicial proceedings. In *Respublica v. Passmore*, a frequently cited case in support of contempt by publication, the Supreme Court of Pennsylvania said the interest in unbiased courts was paramount, that "the streams of justice [must be] clear and pure . . . If the minds of the public can be prejudiced by such improper publications, before a cause is heard, justice cannot be administered."[11]

In the early 1800s, federal judges echoed this theme, but in the highly politicized climate of the Alien and Sedition Act period, judicial concern for unbiased justice takes on a disingenuous character.[12] Federalist judges' abuse of contempt power contributed to the general public distrust of the judiciary's use of the contempt power. In *United States v. Duane*, one of the strands of the tangled web of legal actions brought by the administration of President John Adams against William Duane, the editor of the Philadelphia *Aurora* and an outspoken opponent of the Federalists, federal judge William Tilghman held Duane in contempt for an article critical of Federalist's courts. The judge called for an absolute ban on the discussion of pending litigation in the press.

> If therefore the trial by jury is to be preserved; if the rights of suitors are to be protected touching their dearest interests, of property, life, or character; courts must prevent all discussions, all interference, or reflections in newspapers, while causes are pending.

In the *Aurora* and before the Congress of the United States, Duane claimed the Federalists were violating his right to freedom of the press, but no freedom of the press claim appeared in the case reports.[13]

The passage of the Federal Contempt Statute in 1831 effec-

tively eliminated the power of federal judges to issue summary
contempt citations, but it did not end the judges' efforts to prevent "trial by newspaper." In *Ex parte Poulson*, federal judge
Henry Baldwin bemoaned the passage of the contempt statute
which, he said, "disarmed" the court "in relation to the press,"
and begged the press to "remember that suitors stand unarmed
and defenseless before them; that the hands of the court are
manackled; that the law of 1831 has placed no arbiter between
an editor and a party to a trial, whose life, character, liberty, or
property may be put in jeopardy by the influence of the press."[14]

Judge Baldwin soon found a means to prevent publicity
about ongoing trials. In *United States v. Holmes*, a murder trial
of a sailor accused of throwing shipwrecked passengers out of a
lifeboat in the North Atlantic, he ordered the reporters attend-
ing the trial to not publish any stories until the end of the trial
proceedings. The court reporter observed that the "several sten-
ographers connected with the newspaper press . . . expressed
their acquiescence."[15]

In sharp contrast to the federal bench, the few early reported contempt cases in state courts suggest the strong restraint
placed on courts by the general spirit of freedom of the press.
Judges retained the contempt power, but used it sparingly.

In *People v. Few*, the court "condemn[ed] the publication
in question" but declined to grant an attachment, and in *Ex
parte Spooner* a New York City Grand Jury noted a recent contempt by publication in Baltimore, but declined to hold the
publisher of the New York *Columbian* in contempt. Summary
contempt power was, the court said, "intimately connected with
the liberty of the press," and should only be exercised in the
extreme circumstances.[16]

Ex parte Hickey, *Stuart v. People*, and *State v. Dunham*,
three pre–Civil War cases, stand for a limited interpretation of
the scope of the contempt by publication powers of the judiciary. In *Hickey* a judge presiding over a murder trial fined
Walter Hickey, the publisher of the Vicksburg *Sentinel*, five
hundred dollars for an editorial in which he urged that a sitting

judge "be hurled from a seat he desecrates, and brought as a criminal abettor of murder to the bar, to answer for his crimes." The state supreme court reversed the citation because of the need for "unshackled popular inquiry and discussion"[17] of the judicial process. The court said the state constitutional press clause limited the contempt power, but did not define the freedom of the press in terms of a watchdog role for the press.

> The reflections of the petitioner upon the circuit judge . . . when judged by the practice and assumptions of the English and some American courts, constitute an undoubted contempt . . . but when passed through the crucible of our state constitution, instead of a contempt of court, they become a mere libel on a functionary, and subject only to the punishment prescribed by law for the latter offence.[18]

William Stuart, the publisher of the Chicago *Daily American*, introduced the watchdog into contempt case law. He used it as a justification for a "contemptuous article" in which he criticized the jury and judge in a Cook County, Illinois, murder trial. Stuart responded to the contempt citation by claiming that it was his "duty to inform . . . his readers on matters of a public nature":[19]

> This respondent, in the discharge of his duty as editor of a public journal, is often called upon to animadvert upon public men and measures. This duty he endeavors to discharge free from bias of ill will, malevolence or hatred, fear, favor, or affection. He considers the public acts of public men, in their public capacity, as the property of the people and subject to all reasonable and true examination.[20]

The Illinois Supreme Court dismissed the watchdog role argued by the publisher. It suggested that "an honest, independent and intelligent court will win its way to public confidence in spite of newspaper paragraphs." Libel law where, the court said, a judge "and his assailant should be placed on equal grounds" before a jury, provided the proper remedy for false criticism of individual judges.[21]

An Iowan publisher's willingness to do battle in the pages of his newspaper suggests the strength of tradition of freedom of the press before the Civil War and the precarious position of any judge who challenged that tradition. In *State v. Dunham*, the court's dicta about the power of freedom of the press, and excerpts from a publisher's editorial campaign against a contempt conviction, indicate that the antijudge sentiment in Iowa combined with the tradition of the public's freedom of the press to criticize the courts weakened the contempt power. Following a hearing on a contempt charge for publishing an editorial, Dunham attacked the sitting judge in his paper. In an editorial titled "The First Attempt In Iowa to Muzzle the Press," he promised to "give a full account of this high-handed assault upon the liberty of the press by a vindictive and unjust judge."[22] The next day he took another swipe at the judge.

> At the mere will and pleasure of an unjust and arbitrary judge, in violation of his constitutional rights, the editor of this paper was arrested and carried before Judge Claggett, for daring to express his opinions of the doings of the Circuit Court, in a case already adjudicated . . . the most intense interest has been felt in this community, and Democrats, Republicans — men of all parties — have not only expressed their sympathy, but their determination to see the liberty of speech and the press vindicated, and the petty tyrant who disgraces the judiciary of Iowa, shorn of the power he is now abusing.[23]

The judge issued another contempt citation, to which the publisher responded with additional editorials full of appeals to freedom of the press and attacks on "Judge Claggett [who] constituted himself judge and jury, and would have added the character of executioner if he had dared."[24] A third contempt citation followed.

The state supreme court's observations about the power of
freedom of the press and the position of courts indicated the
vulnerable position of judges who abused the contempt power:

> It would be a fruitless undertaking, in this country — where
> the freedom of speech and press is so fully recognized, and
> so highly prized — to attempt to prevent judicial opinions
> from being open to comment and discussion as an opinion
> or treatise upon any other subject. It is well and fortunate
> that it is so.[25]

The record of contempt case law before the Civil War
shows that contempt did not present a major threat to newspaper publishers after the Alien and Sedition Act period. A general distrust of judicial use of the power and broad public support for freedom of the *public* to criticize judges and the court
system checked the use of contempt power.

In the second half of the century contempts by publication
increased, but newspaper advocates did not use the watchdog
concept of freedom of the press as a primary argument against
judicial "reassertion" of the power of contempt by publication.[26]

Where Was the Watchdog? 1865–1900

Many of the same issues and questions found in late nineteenth-century libel case law appear in contempt case law from
the late 1860s to the end of the century. The case law contains
discussions of newsgathering, the uncertainty over the meaning
of freedom of the press, the public's need and desire for news,
criticism of the sensational press and its reporting of crime
news, and judges' use of the distinction of liberty from licentiousness.

Following the Civil War, two lines of contempt case law
developed. When judges recognized the checking value of
freedom of the press, the contempt power remained limited. In
the other line of cases, judges stressed the need to protect the

administration of justice and upheld broad use of contempt by publication. The watchdog concept appeared in both lines of cases, but is not a significant factor. The watchdog did not fit into the law of contempt as it did in libel. Publishers had little to gain by establishing a special status for the press in contempt. The weakness of the watchdog concept was further undercut by the fact-situations in many cases. Judges resisted watchdog claims when the press sensationalized reports of trials or harshly criticized judges. Using passionate rhetoric, they focused on the public's interest in the protection of the judicial process and paid little or no attention to the watchdog function of the press.[27]

The Tennessee Supreme Court signaled a change in the use of contempt power. In *State v. Galloway*, the court upheld a contempt by publication for an editorial that "denounc[ed] the judge of the [criminal court in Memphis] as guilty of official corruption." Judge Henry G. Smith said, "The power to punish for contempts is absolutely essential to the power and existence of Courts." To be effectual, the judge continued, "the power must be instant and inevitable."[28]

Although Judge Smith acknowledged the public interest in publicity about the administration of power, he asserted that the power to control the publication of information about pending judicial proceedings "must rest largely in the discretion of the judge." Adopting the position taken by Federal Circuit Judge Baldwin in *United States v. Harmon*, the judge suggested that a trial judge could deny access to the courtroom to anyone "there for the purpose of reporting on the testimony or proceedings of the court" unless the reporter agreed to not publish until the end of the trial.[29] The republican tradition of freedom of the press dominated contempt cases before the Civil War, but in *State v. Galloway*, the Tennessee court placed the judiciary's authority to protect judicial proceedings above freedom of the press.

In 1869, the New Hampshire Supreme Court upheld a contempt conviction for a letter printed in a newspaper. The court rejected any special protection for the press and severely limited the area of protected reporting, criticism, or comment about the courts, explaining that

> [t]he publishers of newspapers have the right, but no higher right than others, to bring to the public notice, the conduct of the courts and parties after the decision has been made; and providing the publications are true, and fair in spirit, there is no law . . . to restrain or punish the freest expression of disapprobation that any person may entertain.[30]

The power to hold journalists in contempt when, in the view of a judge, a publication violated his standards of fairness or accuracy, provided wide latitude in the use of contempt power. When combined with the bad tendency doctrine, the contempt power became even stronger.

The Chicago *Evening Journal* editorialized about a pending murder trial in the early 1870s. The paper protested the delay in the trial of "the murderer Chris Rafferty." The public expected, the paper said, that "the hanging of this notorious human butcher would not be delayed for a single day." The *Journal* pointed its finger at the courts as the cause for the delay, claiming that "the courts are now completely in the control of corrupt and mercenary shysters — the jackals of the legal profession — who feast and fatten on human blood spilled by the hands of other men." The publisher responded to a contempt citation by claiming his intention was to act as a watchdog for the public, not to interfere with the court. He claimed the right to "examine the proceedings of any and every department of government" for the purpose of "impress[ing] upon the community the importance of electing members to the next general assembly of the state who would remedy the defects in the criminal law of the state."[31]

But the court held that the tendency of such editorials to interfere with the judicial process was in itself enough of a threat to the judicial process to warrant extending the contempt power to publications that might have a tendency to influence the decision-making process.[32]

The use of a bad tendency standard eliminated any possible utility for the watchdog role. Even if the court had recognized an institutional role of the press as a watchdog over the judicial system, its decision would have remained the same. In contrast, in 1875 the same court reversed a contempt by publication against Wilber Storey, the publisher of the Chicago *Times*.[33] Storey was enmeshed in over twenty libel cases and criminal indictments as a result of stories in which he attacked Chicago public officials.[34] He was held in contempt after he criticized a member of a grand jury. Storey claimed the contempt action violated the freedom of the press, but there is no indication that he argued on institutional grounds.

In reversing the contempt citation against Storey, the court relied, in part, on the state constitutional guarantee of freedom of the press. Because the judiciary was elected and grand juries were appointed by elected officials, the court reasoned, "a necessity exists for public information, with regard to the conduct and character" of judges and members of grand juries.[35]

The court's discussion of the public interest in a watchdog supplying information to the electorate suggests an institutional role for the press, but when the Illinois court's decisions in *People v. Wilson* and *Storey v. People* are compared, the irrelevance of the status of the institutional press is clear. The two lines of contempt cases in the late 1800s turn on judges' perception of the threat to the public interest posed by publicity and criticism of the courts. In 1818 the presiding officer in a New York City grand jury observed that the contempt power was "highly prerogative."[36] In the 1880s and 1890s, judges proved the truth of his observation and the minimal value of the institutional role of press as a public watchdog in contempt cases. When judges felt abused by newspaper reports the watchdog provided little protection.

The West Virginia Supreme Court held the publishers of the

Wheeling *Intelligencer* in contempt for reporting that three members of the court promised the "Democratic caucus" a favorable ruling in a case pending before the court. Chief Justice Okey Johnson's opinion wrapped the judges' reputations in the robes of public interest while at the same time placing the judiciary above the people.

> It will be a sorry day when the practice shall obtain among judges of the court of last resort, who hold the dearest interests of the people in their hands, where in their judicial capacity they may be grossly libeled to leave their high positions and go before a jury in a libel suit, be subjected to the coarse criticism of a defendant's counsel, and if they succeed in their suit, have it cast in their teeth, that they were influenced by sordid motives.[37]

In a concurring opinion, Judge Adam C. Snyder "cheerfully conceded" the right of "public journals to criticize freely the acts of public officials." But he placed narrow limits on the freedom of the press or the public to act as a check on judicial power. "[S]uch criticism," he said, "should always be just and with a view to promote the public good. Where the conduct of a public officer is wilfully corrupt, no measure of condemnation can be too severe, but when the misconduct apparent or real, may be simply an honest error of judgment the condemnation ought to be withheld or mingled with charity."[38]

The Colorado Supreme Court acknowledged a limited watchdog role for the press, but upheld a contempt order against the publisher of the Denver *Republican*. The publisher and other defendants claimed that "as editors, managers and publishers of" a newspaper the freedom of the press gave them the right "to examine, comment upon or condemn publicly . . . the proceedings of any and every department of government." The court agreed, but it said such criticism must be "in temperate and respectful language." The court's description of the interests to be weighed in such cases illustrates the weakness of the institutional-based watchdog concept when it is balanced against the use of judicial authority to guard the individual's right to a fair trial.

> We recognize . . . the inestimable value of a fearless and independent press; but we would be grossly neglectful of our official duty were we, while carefully guarding the independence of the press, to forget the independence of the judiciary which is absolutely essential to constitutional government and liberty.[39]

Using this definition of the interests to be balanced in the use of the contempt power, the Colorado court had little trouble justifying contempt by publication.

In Massachusetts, a contempt order for publishing evidence not admitted at trial resulted in contempt citations against two Worcester newspapers, the *Telegraph* and the *Gazette*. The Supreme Judicial Court did not even mention the freedom of the press in upholding the ruling; instead, the court assumed that the published facts about the case would prejudice the jurors.

> The facts stated . . . if they were brought to the knowledge of the jurors before they rendered their verdict, were calculated to influence them . . . The newspapers were published in Worcester, and it was not improbable at the time of publication that the articles would be read by some of the jurors before the trial of petition was finished.[40]

This view of the question, in which judges portrayed themselves as champions of the people's right to a fair trial against the newspapers' sensational treatment of criminal trials and intemperate criticism of the courts, negated any power the watchdog concept might have had in contempt cases.

But when judges took less adversarial positions in relation to the press, they reversed or refused to issue contempt orders.

> No one ought to be found guilty upon a doubtful charge of indirect contempt, and especially so in a case in any manner involving the freedom of the press. It is true that too

often, under the guise of a guaranteed freedom, the press
transcends the limits of manly criticism and resorts to
methods injurious to persons and tribunals . . . but such
digressions are not always unmixed evils and it is only in
rare instances that [contempt proceedings] can with propriety be resorted to.[41]

An Ohio trial judge refused to issue a contempt citation, stating
that "the abuses of the press are not as dangerous as its suppression would be." He then described the value of the press in terms
of its institutional functions. "The press is a necessary, important, and valuable institution in imparting information with respect to the conduct of every part of government. [It provides]
information to which the people are entitled."[42]

At the end of the nineteenth century, judges who saw the
press as an institution performing an important function in a
representative democracy adopted a view that was in partial
agreement with the liberal tradition articulated by Madison,
Wortman, and other liberal writers at the beginning of the century. They recognized the need for a strong and aggressive institutional press to serve the needs of a watchdog public, and they
acknowledged the importance of the watchdog public as a check
on the judiciary's abuse of its power. But judges who viewed the
press as an adversary departed from the early nineteenth-century tradition of freedom of the press. They asserted the judiciary's authority to determine the public good served by freedom
of the press and used that power to restrain criticism of the
courts. In the effort to combat this aggressive use of the contempt power, the watchdog concept of freedom of the press
proved even less successful than it was in libel cases.

Nineteenth-century contempt by publication placed broad
discretionary power in the hands of judges in state courts. They
had the power to evaluate the public good served by the publication of factual reports and editorial comment about the judicial
process. Judges who recognized the value of the institutional
press wrote that reporting about and criticizing the judicial
process was a "legitimate and proper" function of the press, but

they did not suggest that the public good served by the press required the creation of special protections for the press.[43] In the eyes of nineteenth-century jurists the institutional press all too often practiced "trial by newspaper," and judges refused to give up their power to exercise some control over the press's treatment of the legal process.

Libel and contempt by publication cases presented situations of fact that raised the same freedom of the press issue. The institutional press found itself confronted with common-law requirements that limited the ability of newspapers to publish information about the performance of public officials and the actions of government. In both kinds of cases, the common law dictated the publishers' efforts to define the freedom of the press. In libel they argued for a watchdog concept of freedom of the press because it fit the demands of the common-law libel. But in contempt by publication, the watchdog concept added little to the publishers' defense, and therefore, was not a major factor in contempt by publication case law.

6

A *Watchdog Public*

HE continued failure of nineteenth-century publishers to provide a strong argument for expanding protection of expression in the common law using the concept of a watchdog role of the press demonstrated the weakness of the institutional basis of freedom of the press. Still, twentieth-century free-press advocates have continued to use the watchdog concept in litigation concerning constitutional guarantees of freedom of the press, and judges, not surprisingly, have continued to find little merit in their claims of special protections for the institutional press.

The twentieth-century liberal concept of freedom of the press starts with the assumption that individual expression about matters of public importance is, in and of itself, a public good. This concept began to appear in free-press case law in the late 1910s and the 1920s as federal judges attempted to resolve the free-speech issues raised by government prosecution of anarchists, socialists, and others who espoused unpopular political beliefs in the volatile political climate surrounding World War I.[1] In the radical speech cases of this period, the Supreme Court started to develop a concept of freedom of press based on the inherent value of individual expression in a democracy. Freedom of the press barred government from restricting speech, even speech it believed to be erroneous and of no value to the public, because, Justice Oliver Wendell Holmes wrote, "the best test of truth is the power of the thought to get itself accepted in the competition of the market . . . That at any rate is the theory of our Constitution."[2]

This view of the public good served by individual expression was in marked contrast to the nineteenth-century concept of freedom of the press. Although nineteenth-century common law protected some discussion of public matters, the common law placed the entire burden of proving the value of expression on the speaker. The watchdog concept developed in response to the common-law libel demand that newspapers justify expression in terms of its instrumental value. It was not based on the individual's right to speak but rather on the institutional press's duty to serve the public interest. The development of the watchdog concept was not an attempt to change the common-law concept of freedom of the press. Advocates of the watchdog desired only an answer to the demands of the common law. But as long as the power to determine the value of speech depended on judicial determination of the public good and public good was defined in terms of majoritarian interests, great potential existed for the discovery of improper motives and unjustifiable ends.

Institutional watchdog status would have given publishers both motive and justification for the publication of otherwise unprotected defamatory speech. When confronted with proving proper motive and a justifiable end for libelous statements, a publisher could point to his duty as the publisher of a public journal to inform the public about the performance and character of public officials. In short, judicial acceptance of the watchdog concept would have established the institutional press as the designated protector of the public good. Incorporation of the watchdog concept into common-law libel would have created special protection for the press from libel actions, but it would not have given the press an institutional right to freedom of the press independent of judicial perceptions of the public good.

The watchdog concept accepted the emphasis in the common law on the public good as the primary measure of protected speech. In 1895, an ANPA report on libel law illustrated the institutional press's subordinate status under the watchdog concept of freedom of the press:

> You and I have the right to publish for the public benefit
> . . . because the stability of our government and the happiness of our people will be secured by the publication of the truth, by keeping them informed of their rights and of the dangers to their rights on every hand, by exposing the imposter, by throwing the light of your publication upon the whole field, for the benefit of the masses. That is the justification for a free press, and that is the only justification. You have no right of publication inherent, and that right is justified only by the rights of the public and the benefit of the public.[3]

In that the public good was the basis for publishers' right to freedom of the press, the institutional press could not have an independent right to freedom of the press.

The public good proved to be an arbitrary and often uncomfortably tight measure in the hands of nineteenth-century judges. One judge's aggressive watchdog serving the public interest was another judge's rabid hound spreading poison with every bite. As long as the meaning of freedom of the press was defined by judicial measures of the value of expression, no clear standards existed for setting the limits of protected expression. Publishers used the watchdog to attempt to create protection within the common law, but judges refused to accept the claim of special institutional protection.

Even those judges who applauded the newspaper industry's efforts to shed light on the workings of government refused to grant the industry special status. Judges recognized the importance and need for an organized system of gathering and distributing information, but they did not equate the functions of the press with an institutional right of freedom of the press. When confronted with claims of special privilege, judges throughout the century responded that "in this country *every citizen* has the right to call the attention of his fellow citizens to the malad-ministration of public affairs or the misconduct of public serv-ants, if his real motive . . . is to bring about reform of abuses" (emphasis added).[4]

A WATCHDOG PUBLIC AND THE INSTITUTIONAL PRESS

The institutional press was an addition built onto the tradi-tional liberal, individual-based concept of freedom of the press. Opposition ideology provided the theoretical framework for the American common-law conception of freedom of the press. The combination of a natural right to freedom of expression and deep skepticism about the use of governmental power created the concept of a watchdog *public*. American common law ex-panded to meet the demands of a public watchdog in a constitu-tional democracy, but it did not expand as far as newspaper publishers desired. As newspaper publishing became an industry engaged in the production of news, publishers felt the con-straints of the narrow privileges in common-law libel. Crime news, intemperate criticisms of government officials, and sensa-tionalized treatment of private citizens could not be defended easily under the existing common law.

The watchdog concept responded to the demands of the common law and borrowed from the dominant republican tradi-tion of freedom of the press. Nineteenth-century lawyers did little more than line up precedent in support of industry claims of special protection for the institutional press. The legal climate of the day did not demand an elaborate theoretical discussion of the institutional watchdog; and none was offered. The claim fit the demands of the black letter law, and therefore, it had merit. In contempt law, in which the watchdog claim did not fit the demands of the law, publishers relied on the widely held, strong republican tradition of support for an individual's right to criticize the courts.

The strength of the popular belief in the importance of the individual's right to "think as you will and speak as you think"[5] provided much of the power for a strong liberal concept of freedom of the press. When the individualistic notion of freedom of the press was combined with a healthy skepticism about governmental use of power, freedom of the press became a strong check on government's ability to restrain speech. Tocqueville only slightly overstated the case when he observed that "Nothing . . . is rarer than to see judicial proceedings taken against [the press]."[6] Judicial reluctance to use contempt by publication powers in the first half of the nineteenth century demonstrated the strength of the watchdog public concept of freedom of the press. Judges had the power to hold publications in contempt for interfering with the judicial process, but the strong public support for the right of the individual to criticize and discuss the courts made judges think twice before using the contempt power.

The watchdog concept attempted to transfer the power of the individual-based right of freedom of the press to the newspaper industry. Reporters, editors, and publishers had free-press rights as individuals, but the watchdog concept intended to provide protection for the newsgathering conventions and practices of the newspaper industry. But no evidence exists that the claim captured public support, and judges consistently held that freedom of the press was an individual right.

FREEDOM OF THE PRESS AS A TRUMP

The right to freedom of the press would be stronger if judges decided free-press questions using Ronald Dworkin's statement of a principle of freedom of the press. The basis for determining the limits of freedom of the press should be "the speaker's special position as someone wanting to express his convictions on matters of political or social importance." The right "entitles [the speaker], in fairness, to special consideration, even though the community as a whole may suffer from allowing him to speak."[7]

Nineteenth-century free-press case law demonstrated the danger of viewing freedom of the press as a matter of public policy, rather than as an individual right. Given the opportunity to evaluate free-press claims in terms of the collective good, judges had great discretion to find speech to be in conflict with the public good. The narrow privileges in nineteenth-century libel law and the aggressive use of contempt by publication in the second half of the century indicated the vulnerability of the right to freedom of the press when a weak conception of the right is balanced against judicial perceptions of the public good. The result was severely limited protection of speech and widely divergent interpretations of freedom of the press.

One area in which judicial perception has come into conflict with advocates of free expression is libel law. The tension in libel law between freedom of the press and protection of the reputations of public officials has been an important battlefield in the struggle for freedom of the press in the United States.[8]

In twentieth-century libel law, the Supreme Court attempted, in *New York Times v. Sullivan*, to increase protection of speech at the expense of public officials' reputations. The Court constitutionalized the common law of libel because "debate on public issues should be uninhibited, robust, and wide-open, and . . . it may well include vehement, caustic, and sometimes unpleasantly sharp attacks on government and public officials." The First Amendment "require[d]," Justice Brennan said, that "breathing space" be created for false statements concerning the public officials.[9]

In *Times v. Sullivan*, the Supreme Court found in the federal constitution the protection nineteenth-century publishers had argued the watchdog concept should establish in the common law. Mass media are given greater protection from libel judgments when publishing information about matters of public concern.[10] However, even though constitutional libel law provides greater protection from libel actions than was available under the common law, the history of libel law following *Times v. Sullivan* is dismal. In the last decade, libel has experienced "a rejuvenation."[11] Rather than resolve the seemingly ever-present problems in libel law, *Times v. Sullivan* and its progeny have changed the rules but retained many problems of the common law.[12] In a tone and spirit reminiscent of the late nineteenth century, contemporary critics point to either its "chilling effect" on mass media or the unfair protection given the press to publish falsehoods.[13] Law reviews regularly publish articles warning of the threat of libel litigation or proposals to fix the law of libel.[14]

Justice Brennan's language in *Times v. Sullivan* suggests the fundamental flaw with contemporary libel law. He said the First Amendment existed to protect "debate" and create "breathing space." The Court protected "vehement, caustic and sometimes unpleasant" speech because it served the public interest in the self-governing process. Thus, just as the watchdog concept of freedom of the press depended on the value of expression, *Times v. Sullivan* continued to measure the societal value of discussion rather than protecting as a matter of principle the individual's right to participate in public debate.

Brennan's opinion was based on Alexander Meiklejohn's theory of freedom of the press. Meiklejohn based his theory on what he termed "self-government." In order for a democracy to function, the electorate must have the information needed to make proper decisions about the operation of government. Because Meiklejohn's primary concern was the availability of information, he did not think freedom of the press guaranteed every individual the right to speak: "What is essential is not that everyone shall speak, but that everything worth saying shall be said."[15]

Meiklejohn stressed the importance of protecting a wide diversity of opinion, but his emphasis on protecting only that speech which contributed to the self-governing process eroded the strength of the individual's right to freedom of the press. Whenever protection of freedom of expression is based on the societal value of the speech, whether the value judgment is made by the leader of a traditional New England town meeting, to use Meiklejohn's analogy, or by a judge, the right to freedom of the press is endangered. Meiklejohn's concept of freedom of the press highlights the importance of discussion in a democracy, but it failed to provide a theory for developing strong protections for freedom of the press. In libel law, the Court's attempt to protect discussion has, Floyd Abrams observed, "achieve[d] the worst of two worlds. It does little to protect reputations and much to deter free speech."[16]

The Court attempted to find a satisfactory balance between the First Amendment right to speak on matters of public concern and the individual's right to reputation. But instead of basing its decision on the individual's right to speak, the Court merely adjusted the balance in libel law to give greater weight to the public interest in public discussion. Instead of beginning its analysis of libel from a principle of freedom of speech as a fundamental individual right, the Court developed a policy of freedom of the press based on the public good served by discussion of public matters.

The factual standard of actual malice and the need to determine as a matter of law whether the plaintiff is a public or private figure are intended to give greater weight to speech interests when balanced against reputational interests. But, as Justice William O. Douglas wrote in dissent in *Gertz v. Welch*, the Court's attempt to "define the proper accommodation between the law of defamation and freedoms of speech and press protected by the First Amendment . . . is a quite hopeless one."[17] In practice, although judges use the language of constitutional libel law, judicial decisions in libel cases frequently appear to rely on common-law notions of public good, the motive of the speaker, and the public benefit of the speech in question.[18] Moreover, jury verdicts frequently seem to demonstrate the jury's inability to understand the "virtually unintelligible formulation" of the law contained in instructions received from the bench.[19]

If the First Amendment problems in contemporary libel law were merely a matter of fixing the legal mechanisms used to operationalize a body of law based on a principle of freedom of the press, solutions could be found with relative ease. But the problems in libel are not only at the operational level; the use of a public value standard in creating the constitutional law of libel is the core of the problem in libel law.

When judicial interpretations of freedom of the press pertain to a policy of freedom of the press, the results are difficult to understand or defend because they are based on judicial perceptions of the public good. As the use of the watchdog concept in the nineteenth century showed, policies of freedom of the press are open to widely divergent interpretation.

For example, in *Ollman v. Evans*, a 1984 libel case concerning the fair comment privilege, the Court of Appeals for the District of Columbia developed a new standard for distinguishing protected opinions from unprotected factual statements.[20] The court's opinion said that the First Amendment required that the court change the common-law "accommodation" of freedom of the press and protection of reputation in order to provide greater protection for expression of opinions. Greater protection was required because, Judge Kenneth W. Starr said, the First Amendment protection of freedom of the press required "absolute immunity for all opinions." Opinions required greater protection, he wrote, because even false ideas contribute to "uninhibited, robust, and wide-open debate on public issues." In a concurring opinion, Judge Robert Bork said a new standard more favorable to First Amendment interests was needed because "a freshening stream of libel actions . . . may threaten the public and constitutional interest in free, and frequently rough, discussion."[21]

Free-press advocates hailed the decision as a victory for freedom of the press, but it was a victory built on a weak foundation. Only the result in *Ollman* distinguished this policy-based decision from the policy making of nineteenth-century judges. Nineteenth-century judges narrowly interpreted the fair comment privilege because in their view false ideas harmed public debate. The D.C. Court of Appeals expanded the privilege because a majority of the court placed greater value on the expression of false ideas.

In dissent, Judge Antonin Scalia attacked the majority's view. He said that a statement in an editorial column stating that "Ollman [a college professor] has no status within the profession" was "a classic and coolly crafted libel." Clearly, it served no public interest to protect such charges, he said, "unless it be, quite plainly, the concern that political publicists . . . should be able to destroy private reputations at will." And he described the court's reasoning as "quintessentially legislative."[22]

The Supreme Court denied Professor Bertell Ollman's petition for writ of certiori, but in a dissent to the Court's denial of the petition, Justice William Rehnquist characterized the Court of Appeals decision as an attempt "to solve with a meat ax a very subtle and difficult question, totally oblivious of the rich and complex history of the struggle of the common law to deal with this problem."[23]

The two dissenting opinions illustrate the weakness of policy-based free-press decisions. A question of policy framed the debate between the appeals court's majority and Judge Scalia's and Justice Rehnquist's dissents: How much protection of freedom of the press serves the public interest in political debate? As a result, the opinions focused on the value of the speech in question and on determining how much speech is enough to serve the public interest. A decision based on a principle of freedom of the press would have addressed a more difficult question: If freedom of the press is a fundamental human right, can government regulate speech that serves no perceptible societal interests?

Few would suggest that a principle of freedom of expression should or could be an absolute.[24] Rights exist in societies and ultimately must serve the interests of society. But if freedom of the press is a fundamental part of the bundle of rights in a liberal society, then the right should be based on a principle of freedom of the press, not a policy based on judicial, legislative, or executive perceptions of the collective good.

THE RIGHTS OF THE PRESS

When CBS, Inc. hired David Boies, Jr., a well-known corporate litigator with little experience in First Amendment law, to defend the network in *Westmoreland v. CBS*, many media observers wondered how Boies could possibly grasp the complexities of this special area of the law. His wife, also an attorney, answered, "It's a very short amendment. He will learn it."[25]

When freedom of the press is viewed as a principle, it is indeed a short amendment. It stands for the proposition that each individual has the right to speak out on matters of public concern. The value of that speech is inherent. The very act of speaking out contributes to the public good.

The history of the origins and use of the watchdog is an example of excess baggage being thrown onto the individual-right concept of freedom of the press. Instead of strengthening the individual's right to speak out, the watchdog obscures the strong claim for freedom of the press.[26] It places the press in a position of being an agent of the public interest. As the history of the watchdog shows, an agency role for the institutional press allows courts to constrain press freedom in order to serve the collective good.

The strong argument for First Amendment protection of the watchdog role of the press should be an individual-rights argument. A strong claim to protect the functions of the institutional press can be based on the individual's right to freedom of the press. For example, constitutional protection of the newsgathering function of the institutional press (the area of law in which the watchdog most frequently appears in contemporary case law) is consistent with an individual-right conception of freedom of the press.[27] Citizens have the right to speak out on matters of public concern. In order to intelligently participate in public debate—that is, to fully exercise the right to freedom of speech and press—citizens need access to information and must be allowed to gather that information. The status of a citizen is immaterial. The ultimate use of the information is equally irrelevant. A reporter for the *New York Times* and a curious citizen have an equal right to act as public watchdogs.

Identifying the principle of freedom of the press does not provide an answer for difficult freedom-of-the-press cases, but it does create a framework for constitutional analysis of the right to freedom of the press. Lines still must be drawn to define the relation between an individual's right to speak and other interests. But if judges based free-press decisions on a principle of freedom of the press, a greater burden would be placed on proving a substantial interest in laws that restrict the practice of a fundamental right. In ever-gray areas of free-press litigation, for example, national security and obscenity, judges will continue to weigh the individual right to freedom of the press against other interests. But in the balance, the principle of freedom of the press as a fundamental right in a democratic society should carry greater weight than a policy in favor of expression that serves the public interest.

However, the idea of an institutional watchdog is not worthless, and the institutional press should function as a watchdog. The concept of the citizen watchdog is a powerful component of freedom of the press in the United States. The institutional press's ability to expose abuse of governmental power is critical in modern society. The public has no choice but to rely on the institutional press for information about matters of public concern. But the watchdog function of the institutional press does not create special rights for the institutional press. Claims that the press serves a special function, and therefore requires rights distinct from and greater than the rights granted to individual citizens, open the door to legally defined standards of conduct and responsibility, not stronger rights.

CONCLUSION

The goal of this essay has been to contribute to the understanding of the meaning of freedom of the press in a democratic society. There are three traditional approaches to the legal history of freedom of the press. One, the legal history approach, focuses on appellate court opinions concerning freedom of the press and the legal doctrines developed to address the issues raised in free-press case law. A second approach is concerned with the development of the press as an institution. A third approach examines the history of freedom of the press in colonial and revolutionary America in an attempt to determine the meaning of freedom of the press in 1791, and thereby determine the intent of the framers of the speech and press clauses of the First Amendment.[28]

This study is an attempt to examine the influence of the institutional press on the development of free-press case law and doctrine. As scholars in the field of Law and Society and the Critical Legal Studies movement have stressed, law does not develop in a vacuum.[29] It is the result of competing interests using existing legal mechanisms to achieve desired results.[30] Thus, in order to understand the development of the law of freedom of the press, one must study not only the law but also the forces that shaped the law.

The study of free-press theory provides an analytical framework for sorting out various claims of freedom of the press found in both legal and institutional histories, and in present-day free-press case law. Historical and contemporary journalism and legal literature are full of impassioned and reasoned claims of "freedom of the press." Placing those claims within the context of developed theories of freedom of the press distinguishes the different conceptualizations found under the label of a free press. When, for example, a writer in *Channels* magazine asserts that the First Amendment protects the "media's right to know," free-press theory distinguishes the writer's conceptualization of freedom of the press from a liberal, individual-based concept of freedom of the press.[31]

Press law is unique in that freedom of the press is the only individual right in the federal Bill of Rights with an organized, profit-making, institutional constituency. The watchdog concept of freedom of the press is a direct result of that institutional constituency. The concept supports a claim of special protection for the mass media, and though it is based on a perception of the public interest, only mass media would derive direct benefit from acceptance of the watchdog concept.

This essay focused on a large but relatively narrow sample of the historical material that could be useful in examining the development of the watchdog concept of freedom of the press. Appellate court opinions constituted the majority of the material studied as part of this research. However, excerpts of trial transcripts reprinted in appellate decisions and a small number of examined printed trial transcripts indicate that trial records, either in transcript form or extended reports of trials in newspapers, would shed additional light on the industry's use of the watchdog concept in the law and also on the newspaper industry's adoption of the watchdog concept as an industry convention. Also, the twentieth-century history of the watchdog concept remains unexamined. Given the availability of appellate court briefs and extensive legal literature, a study of the use of the watchdog in the twentieth century should provide valuable information and insight into the influence of mass media litigants on the development of constitutional freedom of the press.

Clifton O. Lawhorne's *Defamation and the Public Official* is an excellent survey of nineteenth-century libel law from an industry perspective, and Norman Rosenberg's recently published study of nineteenth-century libel law, *Protecting the Best*

Men, is a valuable interpretation of nineteenth-century libel law from a critical perspective, but much work remains to be done on the question of freedom of the press and libel law in the nineteenth century. The pressures of libel suits in the 1870s and 1880s led the ANPA and the NEA to call for the passage of state and federal libel statutes. Successful efforts in a number of states resulted in new legislation providing specific protections for the newspaper industry from libel actions. A study of the legislative histories of these statutes would provide valuable information on the use of the watchdog concept in legislative forums. Also, a detailed analysis of the popular and trade press coverage of the industry's efforts to create statutory protection would provide further information about the industry's use of freedom of the press claims.

These studies as well as attempts to examine development and use of other free-press concepts, such as the "right to know," and "the free flow of information," would help to sort out competing and conflicting concepts of freedom of the press.

Freedom of the press is a basic and critical freedom in a free society. We live in a time when the liberal concept of freedom of the press is being severely questioned. Some in the academic community view the liberal concept as little more than the self-serving cry of multinational media corporations; others claim it is an outmoded concept.[32] In the political world, William Casey, the director of the Central Intelligence Agency in the Reagan administration, cited the institutional press's role as the provider of "public information . . . need[ed] to carry out the self-governing process," and then suggested that laws are needed giving the government greater authority to prosecute the press, because there is "too much information that hostile countries can get from the American press."[33] Mr. Casey saw no conflict between his two statements. It is important that those who believe in a principle of freedom of the press make the distinctions necessary to explain the contradiction in Casey's view of freedom of the press, so that we may preserve the power of that principle.

NOTES

CHAPTER 1

1. *Whitney v. California*, 274 U.S. 357, 375(1927).

2. Margaret A. Blanchard, "Filling the Void: Speech and Press in State Courts prior to *Gitlow*," in *The First Amendment Reconsidered*, ed. Bill F. Chamberlain and Charlene J. Brown (New York: Longman, 1982), 14. Blanchard identified over two hundred and seventy cases litigated in state courts before 1925 in which freedom of the press claims were raised.

3. Edward Christion, ed., *Blackstone Commentaries*, vol. 4 (Boston: T. B. Wait & Sons, 1818), 151, 152.

4. Lewis Carroll, *Alice's Adventures in Wonderland & Through the Look-ing-Glass*, ed. Roger Lancelyn Green (Oxford: Oxford Univ. Press, 1971), 127.

5. For example, Floyd Abrams, "The Press Is Different: Reflections on Justice Stewart and the Autonomous Press," *Hofstra L. Rev.* 7(1979):591; Leonard W. Levy, *Emergence of a Free Press* (New York: Oxford Univ. Press, 1985), xii.

6. See Laurence H. Tribe, *Constitutional Choices* (Cambridge: Harvard Univ. Press, 1985), 190. The Supreme Court skirted First Amendment cases in *Ex parte Jackson*, 96 U.S. 727 (1877) and *In re Rapier*, 143 U.S. 110 (1892). In *Patterson v. Colorado*, 205 U.S. 454 (1907), Justice Oliver Wendell Holmes used the Blackstonian definition of freedom of the press to determine the limits of constitutional protection of speech: "The main purpose of such constitutional provisions is 'to prevent all such previous restraints upon publications as has been practiced by other governments,' and they do not prevent the subsequent punishment of such as may be deemed contrary to the public welfare." *Schenck v. United States*, 249 U.S. 47 (1919) is generally considered the first case in which the Supreme Court attempted to determine the meaning of the federal free press clause. See Jeremy Cohen, *Congress Shall Make No Law: Oliver Wendell Holmes, the First Amendment, and Judicial Decision Making* (Ames: Iowa State Univ. Press, 1989).

7. Zechariah Chafee, *Free Speech in the United States*, New Harvard ed. (Cambridge: Harvard Univ. Press, 1942), originally published as *Freedom of Speech*, 1920; Alexander Meiklejohn, *Political Freedom* (New York: Oxford

Univ. Press, 1948); Thomas Emerson, *The System of Freedom of Expression* (New York: Random House, 1970).

8. Michael J. Perry, "Freedom of Expression: An Essay on Theory and Doctrine," *Nw. Univ. L. Rev.* 78(1984):1137; Martin H. Redish, "The Value of Free Speech," *Univ. Pa. L. Rev.* 130(1982):591; Thomas Scanlon, "A Theory of Freedom of Expression," *Philosophy and Public Affairs* 1(1972): 204; Ronald Dworkin, *Taking Rights Seriously* (Cambridge: Harvard Univ. Press, 1978); idem, *A Matter of Principle* (Cambridge: Harvard Univ. Press, 1985).

9. T. Barton Carter, Marc A. Franklin, and Jay B. Wright, *The First Amendment and the Fourth Estate* (Mineola, N.Y.: Foundation Press, 1985), 53.

10. Abrams, *The Press Is Different*, 591.

11. Vincent Blasi, "The Checking Value in First Amendment Theory," *Am. Bar Found. Res. J.* 3(1977):541.

12. For example, Edwin Emery and Michael Emery, *The Press and America*, 4th ed. (Englewood Cliffs, N.J.: Prentice Hall, 1978), xvi; Nick B. Williams, "America's Third Force" in *The Responsibility of the Press*, ed. Gerald Gross (New York: Fleet Pub. Co., 1966), 169; John Hohenberg, *The Professional Journalist*, 3d ed. (New York: Holt, Rinehart and Winston, 1977).

13. Times Mirror, *The People and the Press* (Los Angeles: Times Mirror, 1985), 43; C. T. Hanson, "Gunsmoke and Sleeping Dogs: The Prez's Press at Midterm," *Columbia Journalism Review* (May/June 1983): 27.

14. *Near v. Minnesota*, 283 U.S. 697, 722 (1931).

15. *Sheppard v. Maxwell*, 384 U.S. 333, 350 (1965); *New York Times v. United States*, 403 U.S. 713, 717 (1971); *Saxbe v. Washington Post*, 417 U.S. 843, 868 (1974).

16. Anthony Lewis, "A Public Right to Know about Public Institutions: The First Amendment as a Sword," *Sup. Ct. Rev.* (1980):19; Archibald Cox, "Foreword: Freedom of Expression in the Burger Court," *Harv. L. Rev.* 94(1980):71.

17. Dworkin, *Principle*, 385, 386; idem, *Rights*, 90.

18. *Pell v. Procunier*, 417 U.S. 817 (1974); *Saxbe v. Washington Post*, 417 U.S. 843 (1974); *Houchins v. KQED*, 438 U.S. 1 (1978).

19. Aviam Soifer, "Freedom of the Press in the United States," in *Press Law in Modern Democracies*, ed. Pnina Lahav (New York: Longman, 1985), 79.

20. Alfred McClung Lee, *The Daily Newspaper in America* (New York: MacMillan, 1937), 36.

21. *Abrams v. United States*, 250 U.S. 616, 630 (1919).

22. Chafee, *Free Speech*, 33.

23. William W. Van Alstyne, *Interpretations of the First Amendment* (Durham: Duke Univ. Press Policy Studies, 1984), 60–64.

24. Robert B. Sack, "Reflections on the Wrong Question: Special Constitutional Privilege for the Institutional Press," *Hofstra L. Rev.* 7(1979):629; Redish, "Free Speech," 593, 601–4; Perry, *Freedom of Expression*, 1136; Scanlon, "Theory," 204; Kenneth L. Karst, "Equality as a Central Principle in the First Amendment," *Univ. Chi. L. Rev.* 43(1975):20.

25. Potter Stewart, "Or of the Press," *Hastings Law J.* 26(1975):633–34.

26. *First National Bank of Boston v. Bellotti*, 435 U.S. 765, 798, 801 (1978).

27. *Richmond Newspapers v. Virginia*, 448 U.S. 555(1980); Lewis, "A Public Right to Know," 19.

28. Leonard W. Levy, "The *Legacy* Reexamined," Stan. L. Rev. 37(1985):769.

29. Stephen Botein, "Printers and the American Revolution," in *The Press and the American Revolution*, ed. Bernard Bailyn and John B. Hench (Worcester: American Antiquarian Society, 1980), 11, 22, 32.

30. Ibid., 41.

31. Don R. Pember, "Founders (Meeting in Secret) Protected Our Right to Publish, but Not to Gather the News," *Bulletin of the American Society of Newspaper Editors* (Dec./Jan.) 1979, quoted in Anthony Lewis "A Preferred Position for Journalism?" Hofstra L. Rev. 7(1979): 113, 613.

32. David A. Anderson, "The Origins of the Press Clause," *UCLA L. Rev.* 30(1983):455, 462.

33. Kenneth Schiffler, "Fifty-one First Amendments: State Constitutions and Freedom of Expression," (M.A. thesis, Univ. of Washington, 1985).

34. Charles Miller, *The Supreme Court and the Uses of History* (Cambridge: Belknap Press of Harvard Univ., 1969); also see, Paul Murphy, "Time to Reclaim: The Current Challenge of American Constitutional History," *American Historical Review* 69(1963):77; Morton J. Horwitz, "Progressive Legal Historiography," *Or. L. Rev.* 63(1984):679; Robert W. Gordon, "Critical Legal Histories," *Stan. L. Rev.* 36(1984):57.

35. Harry Kalven, Jr., *The Negro and the First Amendment* (Columbus: Ohio State Univ., 1965), 4.

CHAPTER 2

1. William W. Van Alstyne, *Interpretations of the First Amendment* (Durham: Duke Univ. Policy Studies, 1984), 58.

2. John Milton, *Areopagitica,* 3d. ed., intro. by Sir Richard C. Jebb (1644; reprint, Cambridge: Cambridge Univ. Press, 1940); Frederick S. Siebert, *Freedom of the Press in England* (1952; reprint, Urbana: Univ. of Illinois Press, 1965), 9. "Until late in the eighteenth century freedom of political discussion had a frail history as a broad concept." Leonard W. Levy, *Emergence of a Free Press* (New York: Oxford Univ. Press, 1985), 89.

3. Siebert, *Freedom of the Press*, 21–106.

4. "As the sixteenth century drew to a close, the elaborate structure erected by the Tudors for the control of the press was being subjected to stresses which it could not long withstand." Siebert, *Freedom of the Press,* 103, see also 105–392; "In the mid-sixteenth century, the Crown possessed a wide variety of means for dealing with the printing press including the laws of treason, *Scandalum Magnatum*, heresy, and licensing. Legal restraints and public opinion, how-

ever, gradually forced the Crown to abandon one method after another until in the late seventeenth century it had great difficulty finding a law with which it could defend itself against printed criticism." Philip Hamburger, "The Development of the Law of Seditious Libel and the Control of the Press, *Stan. L. Rev.* 37(1985):662; Bernard Bailyn, *The Ideological Origins of the American Revolution* (Cambridge: Belknap Press of Harvard Univ., 1967), 26–27.

5. Bailyn, *Origins*, 43.

6. Siebert, *Freedom of the Press,* 100, 101.

7. Levy, *Emergence*, 89, 117, 127.

8. *21 State Trials,* quoted in Siebert, *Freedom of the Press*, 392.

9. In the current debate over the meaning of the Constitution, this expectation is described as the search for the "original intent" of the authors of the Constitution. The speech and press clauses of the First Amendment to the Constitution of the United States illustrate the difficulty in determining the intent of the framers. The lack of a well-developed concept of freedom of the press in 1791 illustrates the futility of the view espoused by United States Attorney General Edwin Meese and others to "resurrect the original meaning of the constitutional provisions and statutes as the only reliable guide to judgment" of the meaning of the Constitution. Clearly the language and intent of the framers is important, but the openness of the language of the First Amendment and the lack of a clear understanding of the concept of freedom of the press make the doctrine of "original intent" little more than a political slogan.

10. "A broad term for anything that can affect the general public's finances, health, rights, etc." Daniel Oran, *Oran's Dictionary of the Law* (St. Paul: West Pub. Co., 1983), 341.

11. His essay in favor of liberal divorce laws violated an "Order of the Lords and Commons for the Regulation of Printing," which banned the publication of unlicensed books, papers, or pamphlets. Jebb, Introduction, to *Areopagitica*, xxiii, xxviii. Milton had a personal interest in liberalizing the laws. He wanted to divorce his wife. T. Barton Carter, Marc A. Franklin, and Jay B. Wright, *The First Amendment and the Fourth Estate* (Mineola N.Y.: Foundation Press, 1985), 21–23.

12. Milton, *Areopagitica,* 27.

13. Levy, *Emergence*, 95.

14. Milton, *Areopagitica,* 56–57, 58.

15. Ibid., 47, 64.

16. Bailyn, *Origins*, 27–28; Levy, *Emergence*, 97–100.

17. John Locke, "A Letter Concerning Toleration," in *The Works of John Locke* 11th ed., vol. 6 (London, 1812), 4.

18. Leonard Levy, in *Legacy of Suppression* (New York: Oxford Univ. Press, 1960), argued that "libertarian theory from the time of Milton to the ratification of the First Amendment substantially accepted the right of the state to suppress seditious libel," and that, "the American legislatures, especially during the colonial period, were far more oppressive than the supposedly tyrannous common-law courts." In *Emergence of a Free Press*, Levy retracted the latter claim, acknowledging that "the American experience with a free press was as broad as the theoretical inheritance was narrow." Levy, *Emergence*, ix–xi.

The distinction Levy makes between the theory and the practice of freedom of the press is a valuable one. A number of historical studies of the practice of freedom of the press in colonial and revolutionary America clearly demonstrate broad support for an individual's right to criticize government. See, for example, Gerald J. Baldasty, "A Theory of Freedom of the Press: Massachusetts Newspapers and Law, 1782–1791," (M.A. thesis, Univ. of Wisconsin, Madison, 1974); William F. Chamberlain, "Freedom of Expression in Eighteenth Century Connecticut," in *Newsletters to Newspapers*, ed. Donovan H. Bond and W. R. McLeod (Morgantown: School of Journalism, West Virginia Univ., 1977), 247–61; Jeffery A. Smith, *Printers and Press Freedom* (New York: Oxford Univ. Press, 1988); Dwight L. Tweeter, "King Sears, the Mob and Freedom of the Press in New York, 1765–1776," *Journalism Quarterly* 41(1964): 539, idem, "The Printer and the Chief Justice: Seditious Libel in 1782–1783," *Journalism Quarterly* 45 (1968): 445. Although these studies show that public opinion and practice supported the right to criticize government, they do not show that the public did not accept the authority to punish expression that threatened the public good. The studies show that the public had more liberal notions about the value of speech criticizing the government, not that the public rejected the liberal concept of freedom of the press, which excluded broad areas of expression from the protection under freedom of the press.

19. Bailyn, *Origins*, 47.

20. "[F]ree expression is valuable in part because of the function it performs in checking the abuse of official power." Vincent Blasi, "The Checking Value in First Amendment Theory," *Am. Bar Found. Res. J.* 3(1977):528; Richard Buel, Jr., "Freedom of the Press in Revolutionary America: The Evolution of Libertarianism, 1760–1820," in *The Press and the American Revolution,* ed. Bailyn and Hench (Worcester: American Antiquarian Society, 1980), 71.

21. Bailyn, *Origins,* 35, 43.

22. Buel, "Freedom of the Press," 71.

23. "Of Freedom of Speech," *Cato's Letters,* as reprinted in the *New-York Weekly Journal,* 18 Feb. 1734, in *Freedom of the Press from Zenger to Jefferson,* ed. Leonard W. Levy (Indianapolis: Bobbs-Merrill, 1966), 11, 12.

24. "Reflections upon Libeling," *Cato's Letters,* as reprinted in *New-York Weekly Journal,* 25 Feb. and 4 Mar. 1734, in Levy, *Zenger to Jefferson,* 14, 15.

25. William Livingston, "Of the Use, Abuse, and Liberty of the Press," *The Independent Reflector or Weekly Essays on Sundry Important Subjects,* 30 Aug. 1753, in Levy, *Zenger to Jefferson,* 77.

26. Ibid., 80.

27. Samuel Adams, *Boston Gazette,* 14 Mar. 1768, in Levy, *Emergence,* 67, 117; Alfred M. Lee, *The Daily Newspaper in America* (New York: Macmillan, 1937), 36.

28. See James Morton Smith, *Freedom's Fetters* (Ithaca: Cornell Univ. Press, 1956); John Miller, *The Federalist Era* (New York: Harper & Row, 1960).

29. Levy, *Zenger to Jefferson,* 197–98.

30. *The Virginia Report of 1799–1800.* (1800; reprint, New York: Da Capo Press, 1970), 222, 227.

31. Madison's view of the press as a check on the abuse of governmental

power is frequently cited by twentieth-century advocates of the watchdog concept. However, the nature and role of the press in the late 1700s distinguishes Madison's notion of the checking value of the press from twentieth-century views. In "The Press and Politics in the Age of Jackson," *Journalism Monographs* 89(Aug. 1984): 2, Gerald J. Baldasty states that the press was a means for the opposition political party to check the party in power. "Both Federalists and Republicans used the press in their attempt to marshal public opinion to their policies and ideals. Jefferson believed that newspapers were the key to assuring that true Republicans knew the truth about the Federalist administration and Republican philosophy. The ensuing newspaper debates of the 1790s served to emphasize the political differences that existed and to reify and formalize the two-party division in the 1790s."

32. *The Virginia Report*, 222.

33. Tunis Wortman, *A Treatise Concerning Political Inquiry and the Liberty of the Press* (1800; reprint, New York: Da Capo Press, 1970).

34. Ibid., 25, 26.

35. Ibid., 125, 188.

36. Ibid., 245–46.

37. Ibid., 245.

38. Ibid., 203.

39. Ibid., 161.

40. Ibid., 33.

41. St. George Tucker, ed., *Blackstone Commentaries* 5 vols. (Philadelphia: William Young Birch and Abraham Small, 1803; Shaw Shoemaker Early Am. Imp.).

42. Ibid., vol 1., 2d part, n.G, 11.

43. Ibid., 17, 20, quoting *The Virginia Report*, 220.

44. Ibid., 28, 29.

45. George Sidney Camp, quoted in *The Nature and Tendency of Free Institutions,* ed. Frederick Grimke and John William Ward (1871; reprint, Cambridge: Belknap Press, 1968), 1.

46. Thomas Cooper, *A Treatise on the Law of Libel and the Liberty of the Press* (1830; reprint, New York: Da Capo Press, 1970). See Smith, *Freedom's Fetters*, 303–30; Dumas Malone, *The Public Life of Thomas Cooper* (New Haven: Yale Univ. Press, 1926).

47. Cooper, xxxvii, 40.

48. Ibid., 40.

49. The distinction between government's authority to regulate speech that had a "bad tendency" to harm society and its authority to regulate speech that constituted a "clear and present danger" to society became an important one in the early years of twentieth-century First Amendment case law. Henry J. Abraham, *Freedom and the Court*, 4th ed. (New York: Oxford Univ. Press, 1982), xii, xvii, 209; see also *Schenck v. United States*, 249 U.S. 47 (1919) and *Gitlow v. New York*, 268 U.S. 652 (1925).

50. John S. Mill, "On Liberty," in *Utilitarianism, on Liberty, and Considerations on Representative Government*, ed. H. B. Acton (1859; reprint, New

York: E. P. Dutton, 1976). Mill was not cited in any of the case reports or legal literature examined.

51. Ibid., 75.

52. Ibid., 77.

53. Ibid., 79.

54. Ibid., 112, 114.

55. Zechariah Chafee, Jr., *Freedom of Speech* (New York: Harcourt, Brace and Howe, 1920), 32.

CHAPTER 3

1. Thomas Cooley, *A Treatise on the Constitutional Limitations Which Rest upon the Legislative Power of the States of the American Union*, 2d ed. (Boston: Little, Brown & Co., 1871), 513.

2. *People v. Croswell*, 3 Johns. Cas. 337, 352–53, 357, 358 (N.Y. 1804).

3. Lawrence M. Friedman, *A History of American Law* (New York: Simon and Schuster, 1973), 525–27.

4. Ibid.; Jerold S. Auerbach, *Unequal Justice* (New York: Oxford Univ. Press, 1976), 95.

5. A dictionary definition of the term is given as: "Important legal principles that are accepted by most judges in most states." Daniel Oran, *Oran's Dictionary of the Law* (St. Paul: West Pub. Co., 1983), 55. In common usage, the term implies a concern with *only* the legal rule.

6. Christopher Tiedeman, *A Treatise on the Limitations of Police Power in the United States* (St. Louis: F. H. Thomas Law Book Co., 1886), 189–90; Tiedeman's writing reflected the conservative view of individual rights. He is generally considered one of the most influential treatise writers of the late nineteenth century. James Willard Hurst, *The Growth of American Law* (Boston: Little, Brown & Co., 1950), 338; Clyde E. Jacobs, *Law Writers and the Courts* (Berkeley: Univ. of California Press, 1954), 58–63.

7. See for example, *State v. Van Wye*, 37 S.W. 938 (Mo. 1896), an 1891 statute making it illegal to publish or sell "papers devoted mainly to publication of scandal and immoral conduct" upheld; *Strom v. People*, 43 N.E. 622 (Ill. 1896), an 1889 statute forbidding the exhibition or distribution to minors of publications "devoted to the publication, or principally made up of crime news, police reports, or accounts of criminal deeds, or pictures and stories of deeds of bloodshed, lust or crime," upheld; *Thompson v. State*, 17 Tex. Crim. App. 253 (1884), a conviction of a newsdealer under the Act of 1882, which required state and county occupation taxes totaling $750 "from every person . . . offering for sale the illustrated *Police News, Police Gazette*, and other illustrated publications of like character," upheld.

8. Oran, *Dictionary*, 88.

9. Morton J. Horwitz, *The Transformation of American Law, 1780–1860* (Cambridge: Harvard Univ. Press, 1977), 1; see also 1–31.

10. G. Edward White, *The American Judicial Tradition* (New York: Oxford

Univ. Press, 1976), 114. "As judges began to conceive of common-law adjudication as a process of making and not merely discovering legal rules, they were led to frame legal doctrines based on a self-conscious consideration of social and economic policies." Horwitz, *American Law*, 2.

11. Judges were not alone in this view. Two recent studies of the rise of the popular commercial press in the 1800s, Michael Schudson's, *Discovering the News* (New York: Basic Books, 1978), and Dan Schiller's, *Objectivity and the News* (Philadelphia: Univ. of Pennsylvania Press, 1981) present compelling cases for understanding the content of the commercial press as a reflection of the popular culture. However, the criticism of the press in the elite magazines of the century indicates that many press critics shared the dominant judicial view of the press. For example, "There are unmoral, even immoral gentlemen of the press in this country—men foul-mouthed and impudent, rather than courteous; servers of party—the property of politicians, rather than shields of the Right . . . accepters of bribes, reckless of truth." *Nation* 6(1868): 347; "Murders, suicides, seductions, adulteries, burglaries, thefts, scandals . . . are these not the leading material of a great multitude of our daily papers . . . it is not necessary: it is not on any account desirable." *Scribner's Monthly* 6(1873): 492; "In the early days of journalism there was of necessity a very large ingredient in [the press] of falsehood, because both writers and readers were ignorant and credulous." *Harper's New Monthly Magazine* 49(1874): 269; "American has in fact transformed journalism from what it once was, the periodical expression of the thought of the time, the opportune record of the questions and answers of contemporary life, into an agency for collecting, condensing, and assimilating the trivialities of the entire human existence." *Atlantic Monthly* 68(1891): 689.

12. Hurst, *Growth of American Law*, 267.

13. Friedman, *History of American Law*, 525; Hurst, *Growth of American Law*, 256–57, 266.

14. Friedman, *History of American Law*, 535.

15. For overviews of the growth and nature of legal education in the nineteenth century, see Hurst, *Growth of American Law*, 256–68; Friedman, *History of American Law*, 525–38; see also Gerald W. Gawalt, "Massachusetts Legal Education in Transition, 1766–1840," *The American Journal of Legal History* 27(1983): 27.

16. See Friedman, *History of American Law*, 538–48.

17. White, *American Judicial Tradition*, 2.

18. Friedman, *History of American Law*, 539.

19. Story was an associate justice of the United States, the Dane Professor of Law at Harvard Law School for sixteen years, and wrote nine multivolumned commentaries on the law. He was also an active behind the scenes political figure on both the state and national levels. See R. Kent Newmyer, *Supreme Court Justice Joseph Story* (Chapel Hill: Univ. of North Carolina Press, 1985); James McClellan, *Joseph Story and the American Constitution* (Norman: Univ. of Oklahoma Press, 1971). Cooley served as a judge on the Michigan Supreme Court and as a law professor at the University of Michigan Law School. In addition to his writing on constitutional law, he authored *A Treatise on the Law of Torts* (Chicago: Callaghan & Co., 1879) and numerous other books, as well as

writing opinions during twenty years on the Michigan Supreme Court. See White, *American Judicial Tradition*, 116–18; Norman L. Rosenberg, "Thomas M. Cooley, Liberal Jurisprudence and the Law of Libel, 1868–1884," *Univ. Puget Sound L. Rev.* 4(1980):55, suggests that Cooley's experience as a newspaper editor may have influenced his view of libel law; Gerald T. Dunne, "The American Blackstone," *Wash. Univ. L. Q.* (1963):327; see also idem, *Justice Joseph Story and the Rise of the Supreme Court* (New York: Simon and Schuster, 1970); and Newmyer, *Supreme Court Justice*.

20. Joseph Story, *Commentaries on the Constitution of the United States* (Boston: Little, Brown & Co., 1883). Story continued a series of treatises started by James Kent, chief justice of the New York Supreme Court and later chancellor of New York's state university. Kent and Story shared a common view of the law and were also close personal friends; White, *American Judicial Tradition*, 46.

21. Ibid., 44; McClellan, *Joseph Story*, 162; Perry Miller, *The Life of the Mind in America* (New York: Harcourt, Brace & World, 1965), 215.

22. Story, *Commentaries*, 635.

23. Ibid.

24. Ibid., 642.

25. Ibid., n.1.

26. Friedman, in *History of American Law*, called it "the most important book for its own generation," 545. See Norman L. Rosenberg, *Protecting the Best Men* (Chapel Hill: Univ. of North Carolina Press, 1985), 156–89; Rosenberg, "Law of Libel," 49; White, *American Judicial Tradition*, 109–29.

27. Cooley, *Limitations*, 417, 422.

28. Ibid., 425.

29. Ibid., 421.

30. Ibid., 457.

31. Henry Billing Brown, "The Liberty of the Press," *Am. L. Rev.* 34(1900):321, 323–24.

32. John Roche, "Civil Liberty in the Age of Enterprise," *Univ. Chi. L. Rev.* 31(1963):103, 104.

33. *State v. Van Wye*, 37 S.W. 938 (Mo. 1896).

34. Abraham, *Freedom and the Court*, 213–14. In *United States v. Carolene Products*, 304 U.S. 144, 152 (1938), n.4, Justice Harlan F. Stone, who later was named chief justice, said, in effect, that the individual rights specifically stated in the Bill of Rights required a different standard of judicial review. In cases involving the first ten amendments to the Constitution, judges should require the government to prove the constitutionality of legislation or other action restricting those freedoms. This higher standard of judicial review is counter to the "presumption of constitutionality" that is the standard doctrine of judicial review. Justice Stone stated the preferred position doctrine in the first paragraph of the note: "There may be narrower scope for the operation of the presumption of constitutionality when legislation appears on its face to be within a specific prohibition of the Constitution, such as those of the first ten amendments, which are deemed equally specific when held to be embraced within the 14th [citations omitted]."

Constitutional law scholar Gerald Gunther, in *Cases and Materials on Constitutional Law*, 10th ed. (Mineola: Foundation Press, 1980), 542, states that "The 'double standard' suggested by the footnote . . . has had a pervasive influence. . . . [T]here can be no doubt that the modern Court has been characterized by a notable activism on behalf of fundamental rights and interests outside the economic sphere."

35. "Under the First Amendment there is no such thing as a false idea." *Gertz v. Welch*, 418 U.S. 323, 339 (1974).

CHAPTER 4

1. "Trial of the Case of *Commonwealth v. David Lee Child*, 1828 Term of Supreme Judicial Court of Massachusetts" (Boston 1829), 89.

2. Civil libel suits posed the greater threat to newspaper publishers. Over one hundred and fifty libel actions in the nineteenth century were examined for this study. Of that number only thirty-three were criminal prosecutions. John Stevens, et al., in "Criminal Libel as Seditious Libel, 1916–65," *Journalism Quarterly* 43(1966): 110, found the number of criminal libel prosecutions in the United States increased from 1865 to the World War I period, but again, criminal prosecutions of newspaper publishers constitute a relatively small portion of the number of criminal actions. Norman L. Rosenberg in *Protecting the Best Men* (Chapel Hill: Univ. of North Carolina Press, 1985), 121, found that "By the early nineteenth century . . . civil libel cases, ostensibly private cases, came to replace criminal prosecutions as the most prevalent restraint on political expression."

3. *New York Times v. Sullivan*, 376 U.S. 254 (1964).

4. State libel statutes were enacted as early as the 1820s. The early statutes provided that truth was a defense in criminal actions. Several states passed libel statutes in the 1840s and 1850s. These statutes codified common-law privilege and specifically addressed the problems of the newspaper industry and newsgathering. The Connecticut statute, as described by the state supreme court in *Hotchkiss v. Porter*, 30 Conn. 414, 420 (1862), protected the newsgathering function of the newspaper industry. "The Act of 1855 was . . . enacted to prevent editors of newspapers from being subjected to heavy punitive damages for articles which contained rumors, so generally circulated and credited as to constitute part of the current news of the day, or proper and just criticism upon public men, public measures or candidates for office, or other matters of public interest."

By the late 1880s, the American Newspaper Publishers Association (ANPA) and the National Editorial Association (NEA) were pressing for state libel statutes and exploring the possibility of a uniform federal statute. See *ANPA Annual Minutes, 1890 to 1899*, and *The First Decennium of the National Editorial Association* (Chicago: NEA, 1896).

5. For example, see *U.S. v. Calender*, 25 F. Cas. 239, 258 (D. Va. 1800); *King v. Root*, 4 Wend 113, 133 (N.Y. 1829); *Commonwealth v. Blanding*, 20

Mass. 304, 313 (1825); *Dexter v. Spear,* 7 F. Cas. 624 (D.R.I. 1825); *Commonwealth v. Whitmarsh, American Jurist* 16 (Mass. 1836): 104; *Giddens v. Mark,* 4 Ga. 364, 367 (1848); *Moore v. Stevenson,* 27 Conn. 14, 29 (1858); *State v. Jeandell,* 5 Harr. 475, 480 (Del. 1854); *Smart v. Blanchard,* 42 N.H. 137, 151 (1860); *Foster v. Scripps,* 39 Mich. 376 (1878); *Barr v. Moore,* 87 Pa. 385, 392 (1878); *Morton v. State,* 3 Tex. Crim. App. 510, 515 (1878); *Perret v. New Orleans Times,* 25 La. Ann. 170, 178 (1873); *Rearick v. Wilcox,* 81 Ill. 77, 81 (1876); *Riley v. Lee,* 11 S.W. 713, 715 (Ky. 1889); *Regensperger v. Kiefer,* 7 A. 724, 725 (Pa. 1887); *Metcalf v. Times Publishing Co.,* 40 A. 864, 865 (R.I. 1898).

6. The phrases "public journal," "public journalist," "public newspaper," or "public press" appear from the 1860s to the end of the century. For example, see *Aldrich v. Press Publishing Co.,* 9 Minn. 123 (1864); *Barnes v. Campbell,* 59 N.H. 128 (1879); *Belknap v. Ball,* 47 N.W. 674 (Mich. 1890); *Bigney v. Van Benthusen,* 36 La. Ann. 38 (1884); *Edwards v. San Jose Printing Co.,* 34 P. 128 (Cal. 1893); *Express Printing Co. v. Copeland,* 64 Tex. 354 (1885); *Fitzpatrick v. Daily States Publishing Co.,* 20 So. 173 (La. 1896); *Metcalf v. Times Publishing,* 40 A. 864 (R.I. 1898); *Negley v. Farrow,* 45 A. 715 (Md. 1882); *Peoples v. The Detroit Post & Tribune,* 54 Mich. 457 (1885); *Sanford v. Bennett,* 24 N.Y. 20 (1861); *State v. Schmidt,* 9 A. 774 (1887); *Struthers & Sons v. The Evening Bulletin,* 3 W.N.C. 215 (Pa. 1877); *Upton v. Hume,* 33 P. 810 (Or. 1893); *Wilson v. Fitch,* 41 Cal. 363 (1871).

7. Thomas Cooley, *Constitutional Limitations,* 6th ed. (Boston: Little, Brown & Co., 1890), 523.

8. Joel D. Eaton, "The American Law of Defamation through *Gertz v. Robert Welch, Inc.,* and beyond: An Analytical Primer," *Va. L. Rev.* 61(1975):1362.

9. Harold L. Nelson, *Libel in News of Congressional Investigating Committees* (Minneapolis: Univ. of Minnesota Press, 1961), 5–6; Kathryn Dix Sowle, "Defamation and the First Amendment," *N.Y. Univ. L. Rev.* 54(1979):478–87. In the common law, the good faith misstatement of fact privilege has been recognized by a minority of states. Eaton, "American Law of Defamation," 1362. For an overview of fair comment in the nineteenth and early twentieth centuries, see George Chase, "Criticism of Public Officers and Candidates for Office," *Am. L. Rev.* 23(1889):346; John E. Hallen, "Fair Comment," *Tex. L. Rev.* 8(1929):41.

10. Thomas M. Cooley, *Law of Torts* (Chicago: Callaghan & Co., 1879), 210.

11. John Townshend, *A Treatise on the Wrongs Called Slander and Libel,* sec. 209 (New York: Baker, Voorhis & Co., 1868), 249.

12. *Curry v. Walter,* 126 Eng. Rep. 1046 (C.P., 1796); *King v. Wright,* 101 Eng. Rep. 1396, 1399 (1799).

13. Sowle, "Defamation and the First Amendment," 478.

14. In *Coleman v. MacLennan,* 98 P. 285, 291, 292 (Kan. 1908), the Kansas court conditioned the privilege by establishing an actual malice standard. The privilege failed if the plaintiff could prove that the defendant acted with "actual

evil-mindedness," which could be shown by producing evidence that the defendant was "reckless in making the charge," or "pernicious."

15. *Commonwealth v. Clap*, 4 Mass. 163, 165, 169 (1808).

16. Justice Thomas Cooley's concurring opinion in *Foster v. Scripps*, 39 Mich. 376, 383 (1878) illustrates the public interest rationale of the nineteenth century. "The reason for permitting a privilege of discussion in the case of a city physician [charged with malpractice] must be this; that by operating on public opinion through the means of public discussion, the board having power might indirectly be influenced, and a removal brought about in the case of an unfit officer. But if the discussion proves to be wholly unwarranted by the facts, there is not only grievous private injury, but also serious public injury." Therefore, Cooley reasoned, no privilege existed to protect false statements of fact concerning a public official not running for reelection.

17. See "Critical Notice: A Treatise on the Law of Slander and Libel," *American Law Magazine* 2(1844): 255; Chase, "Criticism of Public Officers," 346; Van Vechten Veeder, "History and Theory of Law of Defamation," *Colum. L. Rev.* 3(1903):546.

18. Vincent Blasi, "The Checking Value in First Amendment Theory," *Am. Bar Found. Res. J.* 3(1977):523, 528; Bernard Bailyn, *The Ideological Origins of the American Revolution* (Cambridge: Harvard Univ. Press, 1967), 55–93; see also idem, *The Origins of American Politics* (New York: Alfred A. Knopf, 1968), 95-109.

19. *Respublica v. Oswald*, 1 Dall. 319, 325 (Pa. 1788).

20. Ibid., 325.

21. Thomas Starkie, *A Treatise on the Law of Slander, Libel and Scandalum Magnatum* (New York: Collins & Harmany, 1832; see also Clifton O. Lawhorne, *Defamation and Public Officials* (Carbondale: Southern Illinois Press, 1971), 39–111.

22. The political press was the dominant newspaper press in the first half of the century. Political parties funded partisan newspapers that served as organs for them. In a time when even relatively small towns had opposing partisan papers, political figures responded in the party papers to charges made by the opposition rather than by filing libel suits. Gerald J. Baldasty, "The Press and Politics in the Age of Jackson," *Journalism Monographs* 88 (August 1984); Rosenberg, *Protecting the Best Men*, 128–50.

23. "A Faithful Report of the Trial of the Cause of Philip I. Archularius and William Coleman . . . " (New York: Sampson, 1807).

24. Ibid., 30. The jury returned a verdict of not guilty, but the law and the trial record appear to be in conflict with the jury's decision.

25. *Root v. King*, 7 Cow. 613, 628 (N.Y. 1827); *Commonwealth v. Lee*, 29.

26. *Root v. King* 7 Cow. 613, 628 (N.Y. 1827).

27. See also *Skinner ads Power*, 1 Wend. 451 (N.Y. 1828); *Arnold v. Clifford*, 1 F. Cas. 1177 (D. R.I. 1835); *Usher v. Severance*, 20 Me. 9 (1841); *Sheckell v. Jackson*, 64 Mass. 25 (1852); *Hunt v. Bennett*, 19 N.Y. 173 (1859); *Matthew v. Beach*, 7 N.Y. Sup. C. 256 (1851); *Tresca v. Maddox*, 11 La. Ann. 206 (1856); *Sanford v. Bennett*, 24 N.Y. 20 (1861); *Cincinnati Gazette Co. v.*

Timberlake, 10 Ohio St. 548 (1860); *Pittock v. O'Neil*, 63 Pa. St. 253 (1869); *Byers v. Martin*, 2 Colo. 605 (1875); *Foster v. Scripps*, 39 Mich. 376 (1878); *Wilson v. Fitch*, 41 Cal. 363 (1871); *Hewitt v. Pioneer Press*, 23 Minn. 178 (1876); *Negley v. Farrow*, 45 A. 715 (Md. 1882); *Bourreseau v. the Detroit Evening Journal Co.*, 63 Mich. 425 (1886); *Bigney v. Van Benthusen*, 36 La. Ann. 38 (1884); *Cowley v. Pulsifer*, 137 Mass. 392 (1884); *Mallory v. Pioneer Press*, 26 N.W. 904 (Minn. 1884); *Metcalf v. Times Publishing Co.*, 40 A. 864 (R.I. 1898); *Arnold v. Saying Co.*, 76 Mo. App. 159 (1898).

28. *King v. Root*, 4 Wend. 113, 133 (N.Y. 1829).

29. *Hotchkiss v. Oliphant*, 2 Hill 510, 513 (N.Y. 1842).

30. *Arnold v. Clifford*, 1 F. Cas. 1177 (D. R.I. 1835).

31. Joseph Story, *A Familiar Exposition of the Constitution of the United States* (New York: Harper and Bros., 1852), 262, 263.

32. "Every freeman has an undoubted right to lay what sentiments he pleases before the public: to forbid this, is to destroy the freedom of the press; but if he publishes what is improper, mischievous, or illegal, he must take the consequences of his own temerity." Thomas Cooley, ed., *Blackstone Commentaries*, 4th ed., vol. 4 (Chicago: Callaghan & Co., 1899), 152; *Commonwealth v. Wright*, 10 *Monthly Law Reporter* 218, 223 (July, 1847).

33. Michael Schudson, *Discovering the News* (New York: Basic Books, 1978); Dan Schiller, *Objectivity and the News* (Philadelphia: Univ. of Pennsylvania Press, 1981), 12–96; *Sheckell v. Jackson*, 64 Mass. 25 (1852).

34. *Hotchkiss v. Oliphant*, 2 Hill 510, 513 (N.Y. 1842); *Fry v. Bennett*, 16 N.Y. Sup. Ct. 200, 223 (1858).

35. *Sheckell v. Jackson*, 64 Mass. 25, 26 (1852).

36. Ibid., 27.

37. *Tresca v. Maddox*, 11 La. Ann. 206 (1856); *Moore v. Stevenson*, 27 Conn. 14, 29 (1858).

38. *Moore v. Stevenson,* n.63; *Van Derverer v. Sutphin*, 5 Ohio 293 (1855). However, in Massachusetts, the Supreme Judicial Court did recognize a more liberal fair report privilege. It expanded the privilege to include "proceedings before all public bodies, and for the publication of those proceedings for the necessary information of the people." The court said a more liberal privilege than existed in England was required in the United States because of the large number of public meetings of all kinds taking place. *Barrow v. Bell*, 73 Mass. 301, 313 (1856).

The privilege to report on the public actions of public officials and about public meetings also was litigated in the 1850s. For example, in *Hunt v. Bennett*, 19 N.Y. 173 (1859), a New York Court of Appeals held that the privilege did not extend to an article accusing a candidate for an appointed office of police justice of having "beaten, with a whalebone cane, a drunken woman, whom he had arrested," because the office was an appointed rather than an elected one.

39. "The Great Libel Case: Report of the Criminal Prosecution of the *News and Courier* for Libeling Sheriff and Ex-Congressman C. C. Bowen: *The State v. F. W. Dawson*" (Charlestown, S.C.: News and Courier Co., 1875), 76.

40. In a survey taken as part of this research of appellate court reports and

available trial court reports, the author found fewer than fifteen reported cases per decade for the period from 1800 to 1869. In the 1870s and 1880s, over thirty reported cases in each decade were found, but in the 1890s the number dropped below twenty cases. See also Rosenberg, *Protecting the Best Men,* 197–204; *The First Decennium of the National Editorial Association,* vol. 1 (Chicago: NEA, 1896); *ANPA Annual Minutes,* 1890–1897.

41. Alfred M. Lee, *The Daily Newspaper in America* (New York: Macmillan, 1937), 717.

42. *Smith v. Tribune,* 22 F. Cas. 689, 691 (N.D. Ill. 1867).

43. *Detroit Daily Post v. McArthur,* 16 Mich. 447, 451 (1868).

44. Ibid., 454, 455. Privilege did not provide complete protection. The defendant could be held liable for estimated, special, and general damages.

45. *Byers v. Martin,* 2 Col. 605 (1875).

46. *McBee v. Fulton,* 47 Md. 403 (1877).

47. *Hewitt v. Pioneer Press,* 23 Minn. 178 (1876).

48. *Storey v. Wallace,* 60 Ill. 51 (1871).

49. *Bailey v. Kalamazoo Publishing,* 40 Mich. 251, 253 (1879); *Heilmann v. Shanklin,* 60 Ind. 424 (1878).

50. *Storey v. Wallace,* 60 Ill. 51, 57 (1871).

51. Ibid., 54.

52. *Marks v. Baker,* 9 N.W. 678 (Minn. 1881).

53. *Miner v. Post Tribune,* 49 Mich. 358, 364 (1882).

54. *Press Co. v. Stewart,* 14 A. 51, 53 (Pa. 1888).

55. *Bourreseau v. the Detroit Evening Journal Co.,* 63 Mich. 425, 427–28, 429, 432 (1886).

56. *Atkinson v. Detroit Press,* 46 Mich. 341, 383 (1881).

57. *Scripps v. Reilly,* 38 Mich. 10, 22, 27, 28 (1878)

58. *Foster v. Scripps,* 39 Mich. 376, 383 (1878).

59. *Scripps v. Foster,* 41 Mich. 742, 745 (1879). The case first went to the state supreme court on an appeal of a directed verdict for the defendant, James E. Scripps, the publisher of the Detroit *Evening News.* The supreme court overturned the verdict and remanded the case for trial. After a jury verdict for the plaintiff, Scripps appealed on several points, including a claim of privilege.

60. *Bailey v. Kalamazoo Publishing Co.,* 40 Mich. 251, 257 (1879).

61. *Bathrick v. Detroit Post & Tribune Co.,* 50 Mich. 629, 639 (1883).

62. *McAllister v. Detroit Free Press,* 76 Mich. 338, 348–50, 355 (1889).

63. Ibid., 355, 356.

64. *Wilson v. Fitch,* 41 Cal. 363, 364, 383 (1871).

65. *Struthers & Sons v. the Evening Bulletin,* 3 W. N.C. 215 (Pa. 1877).

66. Ibid., 217, 218.

67. *Edwards v. Kansas City Times,* 32 F. 813, 818 (W. D.Mo. 1887).

68. *Neeb v. Hope,* 17 W. N.C. 93 (Pa. 1885).

69. *Negley v. Farrow,* 60 Md. 158, 160, 177 (1882).

70. John Townshend, *A Treatise on the Wrongs Called Slander and Libel,* 4th ed. (New York: Baker, Voorhis & Co., 1890), 445–46.

71. *Barnes v. Campbell,* 59 N.H. 128, 129 (1879).

72. *Regensperger v. Kiefer,* 7 A. 724, 725 (Pa. 1887).

73. *Riley v. Lee,* 11 S.W. 713, 715 (Ky. 1889).

74. *Edwards v. San Jose Printing Co.,* 34 P. 128, 129, 130 (Cal. 1893).

75. *Arnold v. Saying Co.,* 76 Mo. App. 159, 165 (1898).

76. *Ex parte Barry,* 25 P. 256, 608 (1890).

77. *Fitzpatrick v. Daily State Publishing,* 20 So. 173, 174, 176 (1896).

78. Ibid., 178, 181.

79. *Upton v. Hume,* 33 P. 810, 811 (1893).

80. *Metcalf v. Times Publishing Co.,* 40 A. 864, 865 (R.I. 1898).

81. *New York Times v. Sullivan,* 376 U.S. 254, 272 (1964), quoting *NAACP v. Button,* 371 U.S. 415 (1963).

CHAPTER 5

1. Walter Nelles and Carol Weiss King, "Contempt by Publication in the United States: To the Federal Contempt Statute," *Colum. L. Rev.* 28(1928):401, 404–6.

2. Perry Miller, *The Life of the Mind in America* (New York: Harcourt, Brace & World, 1965), 99–116; Gerard W. Gawalt, "Sources of Anti-Lawyer Sentiment in Massachusetts, 1740–1840," *American Journal of Legal History* 14 (1969): 283; *Ex parte Spooner,* 5 City H. Rec. 109, 112 (N.Y. Ct. Gen. Sess. 1820).

3. Sir John Fox, *History of Contempt of Court* (Oxford: Clarendon Press, 1927), 21; *Blackstone Commentaries,* Thomas Cooley, ed., 4th ed., vol 2 (Chicago: Callaghan & Co., 1899), 1439; *The King v. Almon,* Wilm. 243 (1765); Fox, *Contempt of Court,* 20–21.

4. Charles Chauncey, "Contempt of Court," *American Law Register* 20(1881): 220; contra, see James Paterson, *The Liberty of the Press, Speech, and Public Worship* (London: Macmillan & Co., 1880), 121–32.

5. Stewart Rapalje, *A Treatise on Contempt* (New York: L. K. Strouse & Co., 1890), 70; Cromwell H. Thomas, *Problems of Contempt of Court* (Baltimore: Author, 1934), iii.

6. Rapalje, *Contempt,* 71.

7. Samuel Merrill, *Newspaper Libel* (Boston: Ticknor & Co., 1888), 128.

8. Nelles, *Contempt by Publication,* 409–15, 430–31, 531, 534.

9. "The first requisite of a court of justice is, that its machinery be left undisturbed; and this cannot be effected, unless comments be all but excluded till the court has discharged its function. . . . The same power to commit summarily for contempt all persons who intrude into the judicial function . . . is thus deemed inherent in all courts of record." Paterson, *Liberty of the Press,* 122, 535–36.

10. *Stuart v. People,* 4 Ill. 395 (3 Scam. 1842).

11. *Respublica v. Passmore,* 3 Yeates 440, 441 (Pa. 1802).

12. James Morton Smith, *Freedom's Fetters* (Ithaca: Cornell Univ. Press, 1956), 22–35.

13. *United States v. Duane*, 25 F. Cas. 920, 921 (Pa. Crt. Ct. 1801); Smith, *Freedom's Fetters*, 277–306.

14. *Ex parte Poulson*, 19 F. Cas. 1205, 1208, 1209 (E. D. Pa. 1835).

15. *United States v. Holmes*, 26 F. Cas. 360, 363 (E. D. Pa. 1842).

16. *People v. Few*, 2 Johns. 290, 292 (N.Y. 1807); City H. Rec. 109, 111, 112 (1820).

17. *Ex parte Hickey*, 4 S & M 751, 758 (Miss. 1844); *Stuart v. People*, 395; *State v. Dunham*, 6 Iowa 245 (1857).

18. *Ex parte Hickey*, 782.

19. *Stuart v. People*, 395, 396, 399.

20. Ibid., 399.

21. Ibid., 405.

22. *State v. Dunham*, 245, 247.

23. Ibid.

24. Ibid., 249.

25. Ibid., 257.

26. Nelles, *Contempt by Publication*, 535.

27. The longest and most passionate opinions appear in cases concerning criticism of individual judges. Judges took great pains to justify and support use of summary contempt power in situations in which the potential abuse of the power was greatest. Frequently the length and passion of many of the opinions suggest that judges were aware of their own questionable use of contempt power. See Nelles, *Contempt by Publication*, 544–45.

28. *State v. Galloway*, 5 Caldwell 326, 331, 339 (Tenn. 1868).

29. Ibid., 339–40.

30. *In re Sturoc*, 48 N.H. 428, 432 (1869).

31. *People v. Wilson*, 64 Ill. 195, 198, 200 (1872).

32. Ibid., 214.

33. *Storey v. People*, 79 Ill. 45 (1875).

34. Justin E. Walsh, *To Print the News and Raise Hell* (Chapel Hill: Univ. of North Carolina Press, 1968), 238–53.

35. *Storey v. People*, 45, 52–53.

36. *In re Van Hook*, 3 City H. Rec. 64, 65 (1818).

37. *State v. Frew & Hart*, 24 W.Va. 416, 419, 429 (1884).

38. Ibid., 478.

39. *Cooper v. People ex rel. Wyatt*, 22 P. 790, 794–95, 801 (Colo. 1889).

40. *Telegram Newspaper Co. v. Commonwealth*, 52 N.E. 445 (Mass. 1899).

41. *Cheadle v. State*, 11 N.E. 426, 432 (1886).

42. *In re Press-Post*, 3 Ohio N.P. 180 (1894).

43. *Fishback v. State*, 30 N.E. 1088, 1091 (1892).

CHAPTER 6

1. See generally Paul L. Murphy, *The Constitution in Crisis Times, 1918–1969* (New York: Harper & Row, 1972); Robert K. Murray, *Red Scare* (Minneapolis: Univ. of Minnesota Press, 1955); Zechariah Chafee, *Free Speech in the*

United States (Cambridge: Harvard Univ. Press, 1920); H. C. Peterson and Gilbert C. Fite, *Opponents of War, 1917–1918* (Madison: Univ. of Wisconsin Press, 1957).

2. See *Schneck v. United States*, 249 U.S. 47 (1919); *Debs v. United States*, 249 U.S. 211 (1919); *Frohwerk v. United States*, 249 U.S. 204 (1919); *Abrams v. United States*, 250 U.S. 616, 630 (1919); *Gitlow v. New York*, 268 U.S. 325 (1925); *Whitney v. California*, 274 U.S. 357 (1927).

3. Azel F. Hatch quoted in Minutes of American Newspaper Publishers Association's 1895 Annual Meeting, *ANPA Annual Minutes 1890 to 1899*, 72–73.

4. *Palmer v. City of Concord*, 48 N.H. 211, 216 (1868).

5. *Whitney v. California*, 274 U.S. 357 (1927).

6. Alexis de Tocqueville, *Democracy in America*, ed. J. P. Mayer (New York: Anchor Books, 1969), 182–83.

7. Ronald Dworkin, *A Matter of Principle* (Cambridge: Harvard Univ. Press, 1985), 386.

8. See generally Levy, *Emergence of a Free Press*; Clifton O. Lawhorne, *Defamation and Public Officials* (Carbondale: Southern Illinois Univ. Press, 1971); Norman Rosenberg, *Protecting the Best Men* (Chapel Hill: Univ. of North Carolina Press, 1985).

9. *New York Times v. Sullivan*, 376 U.S. 254, 264, 272 (1964); Brennan is quoted from *NAACP v. Button*, 371 U.S. 415, 433 (1963).

10. Under *Times v. Sullivan* a public official bringing a libel suit against a mass media defendant must show that the defendant acted with "actual malice," which the Court defined as "knowledge of falsity or reckless disregard for the truth." In subsequent cases the Court expanded the burden of a fault requirement to all plaintiffs, and prohibited the awarding of punitive damages absent a finding of actual malice. In 1986, the Court ruled that the First Amendment required that the plaintiff in libel actions, in which the speech in question dealt with "matters of public concern," must prove the falsity of the defamation. Important cases in the Supreme Court's effort to make sense of libel law include, *Rosenblatt v. Baer*, 383 U.S. 75 (1966), *Curtis Publishing v. Butts*, 388 U.S. 130 (1967), *Rosenbloom v. Metromedia, Inc.*, 403 U.S. 29 (1971), *Gertz v. Robert Welch, Inc.*, 418 U.S. 323 (1974); *Dun & Bradstreet, Inc. v. Greenmoss Builders, Inc.*, 105 S. Ct. 2939 (1985), *Hepp v. Philadelphia Newspapers*, 475 U.S. 767 (1986); Frank G. Houdek, "Constitutional Limitations on Libel Actions: A Bibliography of *New York Times v. Sullivan* and Its Progeny, 1964–1984," *Comm/Ent L. J.* 6(1984):447, provides a good bibliography of law review articles dealing with libel law since 1964.

11. Rodney A. Smolla, "Let the Author Beware: The Rejuvenation of the American Law of Libel," *Univ. Penn. L. Rev. 132(1983):1*. For an extended discussion of recent major libel cases, see Smolla, *Suing the Press* (New York: Oxford Univ. Press, 1986).

12. "Having spent two years collecting and analyzing information on libel litigation against the press, we have concluded that the failure of libel law to reflect the realities that exist in libel litigation accounts in large part for the problems that are misperceived about libel suits today. . . . Finally, the constitu-

tional privileges—which require a showing of fault as a precondition to recovery—do not protect the press from unwarranted liability nor safeguard interests in freedom of expression. The privileges do not limit recovery only to cases in which liability can be found consistent with freedom of expression. Instead the privileges have required that courts become the primary, if not exclusive, judges of press responsibility. The privileges have fostered a legal action for enforcement of press responsibility, not libel." Randall P. Bezanson, "Libel Law and the Realities of Litigation: Setting the Record Straight," *Iowa L. Rev.* 71(1985):227.

13. "I am concerned that the Westmoreland case and other recent thrusts against the press could too easily lead to a diminution of the effort on the part of the press [to perform as a watchdog]." Floyd Abrams, quoted in, Esther Davidowitz and Mitchell Stephens, "Floyd Abrams: The Lawyer with Press Appeal," *Washington Journalism Review* (Apr. 1985), 41. For an overview of the "chilling effect" claim, see Michael Massing, "The Libel Chill; How Cold *Is* It Out There?" *Columbia Journalism Review* (May/June 1985), 31–43; "The Libel Front," *Columbia Journalism Review* (Jan./Feb. 1986), 35–43. Four discussions of the problems in libel law are, Floyd Abrams, "Why We Should Change the Libel Law," *New York Times Magazine*, 29 Sept. 1985, 34; Anthony Lewis, "Annals of Law: The Sullivan Case," *New Yorker*, 5 Nov. 1984, 52; Renata Adler, *Reckless Disregard* (New York: Knopf, 1986), 34; Robert F. Nagel, "How to Stop Libel Suits and Still Protect Individual Reputation," *Washington Monthly*, 17 Nov. 1985, 12.

14. Among the more valuable law review articles are, Marc A. Franklin, "Winners and Losers and Why: A Study of Defamation Litigation," *Am. Bar Found. Res. J.* (1980):795; idem., "Suing the Media for Libel: A Litigation Study," *Am. Bar Found. Res. J.* (1981):455; and idem, "Good Names and Bad Law: A Critique of Libel Law and a Proposal," *Univ. San Fran. L. Rev.* 18(1983):1; David Anderson, "Reputation, Compensation, and Proof," *Wm. and Mary L. Rev.* 25(1984):747; Rodney Smolla, "Let the Author Beware: The Rejuvenation of the American Law of Libel," *Univ. Penn. L. Rev.* 132:(1983):1; William W. Van Alstyne, "First Amendment Limitations on Recovery from the Press—An Extended Comment on the 'Anderson Solution,'" *Wm. and Mary L. Rev.* 24(1984):793; Anthony Lewis, *"New York Times v. Sullivan* Reconsidered: Time to Return to 'The Central Meaning of the First Amendment,'" *Colum L. Rev.* 83(1983):603; Randall P. Bezanson, Gilbert Cranberg, and John Soloski, "Libel Law and the Press: Setting the Record Straight," *Iowa L.* Rev. 71(1985):215.

15. Alexander Meiklejohn, *Political Freedom* (New York: Oxford Univ. Press, 1948), 9, 26; Harry Kalven, Jr., "The *New York Times* Case: A Note on 'The Central Meaning of the First Amendment,'" *Sup. Ct. Rev.* 209 (1964); Lewis, "New York Times v. Sullivan Reconsidered," 608.

16. Meiklejohn, *Political Freedom*, 24–25; Abrams, "Why We Should Change the Libel Law," 34.

17. *Gertz v. Welch*, 418 U.S. 323, 355–56 (1974).

18. See, for example, *Tavoulareas v. Washington Post*, 759 F. 2d. 90 (C.A. D.C. 1985). The trial jury found in favor of the Plaintiff, but the trial judge

overturned the verdict stating that "there was no evidence in the record" that the article contained "knowing lies or statements made in reckless disregard of the truth." On appeal, the Court of Appeals reversed the trial judge and reinstated the trial jury's verdict. In an eighty-eight page opinion, Judge George E. Mac-Kinnon said there was "evidence . . . sufficient to demonstrate that the article was published in reckless disregard of the truth." The judge stressed the intent of the *Washington Post* as a "muckraking" journal to seek out scandal. The case is pending a rehearing *en banc*, and it is expected it will be appealed to the Supreme Court regardless of the outcome before the D.C. Court of Appeals. The jury is believed to have completely ignored the actual malice standard in reaching its verdict. See Smolla, *Suing the Press*, 182–97.

Two cases illustrate the confusion over the "public figure" standard. In *Griffin v. Kentucky Post*, 10 M.L.R. (BNA) 605 (Ky. Crt. Ct. 1983), a trial judge ruled that an "entertainer who performed regularly as a nude or semi-nude dancer" was a limited public figure. But in *Milkovich v. News-Herald*, 473 N.E. 2d. 1191 (Ohio Sup. Ct. 1984), the Ohio Supreme Court held that a well-known high school wrestling coach was not a limited public figure.

19. Renata Adler, "Annals of Law: 'Two Trials," *The New Yorker* (16 June 1986), 47; reprinted in *Reckless Disregard* (New York: Knopf, 1986).

Adler, "Two Trials," 47.

20. *Ollman v. Evans*, 750 F. 2d. 970 (C.A. D.C. 1984). "First, a court should analyze 'the common usage or meaning of the specific language' used in the challenged statement. . . . Second, a court should consider whether the statement is 'objectively capable of proof or disproof'. . . . Third, a court should examine the immediate context in which the statement is made. 'The language of the entire column may signal that a specific statement which, standing alone, would appear to be factual is in actuality a statement of opinion.' Finally, the court should examine 'the broader social conventions or customs inherent in different types of writing.' " *Karp v. Hill and Knowlton*, 12 M.L.R. (BNA) 2092, 2096 (D.C. S.N.Y. 1986), quoting *Ollman v. Evans*, 750 F. 2d. 970 (1984).

21. *Ollman v. Evans*, 750 F. 2d. 970, 974, 996 (1984); idem., quoting *New York Times v. Sullivan*, 376 U.S. 254, 270 (1964).

22. On 18 June 1986, President Ronald Reagan nominated Judge Scalia to be an associate justice of the United States; *Ollman v. Evans*, 1032, 1036, 1037, 1038.

23. On 18 June 1986, President Ronald Reagan nominated Justice Rehnquist to replace Chief Justice Warren Burger; *Ollman v. Evans*, 86 L. Ed. 2d. 278, 280 (1985).

24. Supreme Court Justices William O. Douglas and Hugo Black are generally identified as absolutists. But both justices, though they asserted that the First Amendment was an absolute, managed to draw distinctions that removed some expression from under the protection of freedom of speech and press. For example, in *Cohen v. California*, 403 U.S. 15 (1971) Justice Black joined a dissent that distinguished "conduct" from "speech." For an example of Douglas's absolutist position, see *Gertz v. Welch*, 418 U.S. 323, 356–57 (1974). Justice

Douglas wrote, "The First Amendment would bar Congress from passing any libel law. . . . With the First Amendment made applicable to the States through the Fourteenth, I do not see how States have any more ability to 'accommodate' freedoms of speech or of the press than does Congress."

25. *Westmoreland v. CBS*, 10 M.L.R. (BNA) 2417 (S.D.N.Y. 1984). General Westmoreland withdrew his libel action four months into the highly publicized trial. See "Press Cautiously Hails Westmoreland's Withdrawal of Libel Suit," *New York Times*, 19 Feb. 1985, 11; "Texts of Statements on the End of Westmoreland's Libel Suit against CBS," *New York Times*, 19 Feb. 1985, 20; Maureen Dowd, "Most of Westermoreland Jury Seemed to Favor CBS, but Doubts Remained," *New York Times*, 20 Feb. 1985, 13; M. A. Farber, "A Joint Statement Ends Libel Action by Westmoreland," *New York Times*, 19 Feb. 1985, 1; Smolla, *Suing The Press*, 198–237; Boies's wife quoted in Cary Reich, "The Litigator," *New York Times Magazine*, 1 June 1986, 48–49.

26. Freedom of the press is one of few individual rights in which serious claims have been made that the primary reason for protecting the right is the collective good. For example, institutional religion is an important individual right with a history that is closely tied to freedom of expression. Yet the individual rights basis for freedom of religion is quite clear. The separation of church and state presented a number of difficult constitutional problems, but no one claims that institutional religion has or should have a greater right to freedom of religion than is granted under the individual's right to hold and practice religious beliefs.

27. See, for example, the prison access cases, *Pell v. Procunier*, 417 U.S. 817 (1974), *Saxbe v. Washington Post*, 417 U.S. 843 (1974), *Houchins v. KQED*, 438 U.S. 1 (1978).

28. For example, Blanchard, "Filling the Void: Speech and Press in State Courts prior to *Gitlow*," in *The First Amendment Revisited*, ed. Chamberlain and Brown (New York: Longman, 1982); Paul L. Murphy, *The Meaning of Freedom of Speech* (Westport, Conn.: Greenwood Pub. Co., 1972); J. Edward Gerald, *The Press and the Constitution, 1931–1947* (Minneapolis: Univ. of Minnesota Press, 1948). Most historical treatments of individual newspapers or publishers discuss the freedom of the press from an industry perspective. The subject is usually not given a great deal of attention unless the publisher or newspaper championed the freedom of the press in response to a specific challenge. Fred W. Friendly, *Minnesota Rag* (New York: Random House, 1981), is one of a very few institutional histories that focus on a publisher's involvement in a free-press question. For early America see, for example, Levy, *Emergence of a Free Press*; Bernard Bailyn, *The Ideological Origins of the American Revolution* (Cambridge: Belknap Press of Harvard Univ., 1967).

29. For discussions of the relation of law to society and the "new legal history," see Robert W. Gordon, "Critical Legal Histories," *Stan. L. Rev.* 36(1984):57; idem, "Introduction: J. Willard Hurst and the Common Law Tradition in American Legal Historiography," *Law and Soc. Rev.* 10(1975):9; Morton J. Horwitz, "The Conservative Tradition in the Writing of American Legal History," *American Journal of Legal History* 17(1973): 275; idem, "Progressive

Legal History," *Or. L. Rev.* 63(1984):679; G. Edward White, "Truth and Interpretation in Legal History," *Mich. L. Rev.* 79(1981):594; idem, "The Inevitability of Critical Legal Studies," *Stan. L. Rev.* 36(1984):649; Paul Murphy, "Time to Reclaim: The Current Challenge of American Constitutional History," *American Historical Review* 69(1963):64; Wythe Holt, "Now and Then: The Uncertain State of Nineteenth-Century American Legal History," *Ind. L. Rev.* 7(1974):615; A. E. Keir Nash, "In Re Radical Interpretations of American Law: The Relation of Law and History," *Mich. L. Rev.* 82(1983):274.

30. Rosenberg, *Protecting the Best Men,* 6–11.

31. Joseph Vitale, "Code of Silence," *Channels* (June 1986): 7.

32. See, for example, Herbert I. Schiller, *Who Knows: Information in the Age of the Fortune 500* (Norwood, N.J.: Ablex Pub. Co., 1981), 21; Stanley Ingber, "The Marketplace of Ideas: A Legitimizing Myth," *Duke L. J.* (1984):1; Mark Tushnet, "Corporations and Free Speech," in *The Politics of Law,* ed. David Kairys (New York: Pantheon Books, 1982), 253.

33. Katherine Winton Evans, "National Security and the Press," *Washington Journalism Review* (July 1986): 16–17.

BIBLIOGRAPHY

EIGHTEENTH- AND NINETEENTH-CENTURY REPORTED COURT CASES

Aldrich v. Press Publishing Co., 9 Minn. 123 (1864).
Arnold v. Clifford, 1 F. Cas. 1177 (D. R.I. 1835) (No. 555).
Arnold v. Saying Co., 76 Mo. App. 159 (1898).
Atkinson v. Detroit Press, 46 Mich. 341 (1881).
Bailey v. Kalamazoo Publishing, 40 Mich. 251 (1879).
Barber v. St. Louis Dispatch Co., 3 Mo. App. 377 (1877).
Barnes v. Campbell, 59 N.H. 128 (1879).
Barr v. Moore, 87 Pa. 385 (1878).
Barrow v. Bell, 73 Mass. 301 (1856).
Bathrick v. Detroit Post & Tribune Co., 50 Mich. 629 (1883).
Belknap v. Ball, 47 N.W. 674 (Mich. 1890).
Bigney v. Van Benthusen, 36 La. Ann. 38 (1884).
Bourreseau v. The Detroit Evening Journal Co., 63 Mich. 425 (1886).
Byers v. Martin, 2 Colo. 605 (1875).
Cheadle v. State, 11 N.E. 426, 432 (Ind. 1886).
Cincinnati Gazette Co. v. Timberlake, 10 Ohio St. 548 (1860).
Commonwealth v. Clap, 4 Mass. 163 (1808).
Commonwealth v. Wright, 10 M. L. R. 218 (Mass. 1847).
Cooper v. People ex rel Wyatt, 22 P. 790 (Colo. 1889).
Cowley v. Pulsifer, 137 Mass. 392 (1884).
Curry v. Walter, Eng. Rep. 1046 (C.P. 1796).
Detroit Daily Post v. McArthur, 16 Mich. 447 (1868).
Edwards v. Kansas City Times, 32 F. 813 (W.D.Mo. 1887).
Edwards v. San Jose Printing Co., 34 P. 128 (Cal. 1893).
Ex parte Barry, 85 Cal. 603, 25 P. 256 (1890).
Ex parte Hickey, 4 S & M 751 (Miss. 1844).
Ex parte Jackson, 96 U.S. 727 (1877).
Ex parte Poulson, 19 F. Cas. 1205 (E. D. Pa. 1835) (No. 11,350).

Ex parte Spooner, 5 City H. Rec. 109 (N.Y. Ct. Gen. Sess. 1820).
Fishback v. State, 30 N.E. 1088, 1091 (Ind. 1892).
Fitzpatrick v. Daily State Publishing, 20 So. 173 (La. 1896).
Foster v. Scripps, 39 Mich. 376 (1878).
Fry v. Bennett, 16 N.Y. Sup. Ct. 200 (1858).
Heilmann v. Shanklin, 60 Ind. 424 (1878).
Hewitt v. Pioneer Press, 23 Minn. 178 (1876).
Hotchkiss v. Oliphant, 2 Hill 510 (N.Y. 1842).
Hunt v. Bennett, 19 N.Y. 173 (1859).
In re Press-Post, 3 Ohio N.P. 180 (1894).
In re Rapier, 143 U.S. 110 (1892).
In re Sturoc, 48 N.H. 428 (1869).
In re Van Hook, 3 City H. Rec. 64 (1818).
Kalamazoo Publishing Co., 40 Mich. 251 (1879).
King v. Root, 4 Wend. 113, 133 (N.Y. 1829).
Kinyon v. Palmer, 18 Iowa 327 (1865).
McAllister v. Detroit Free Press, 76 Mich. 338 (1889).
McBee v. Fulton, 47 Md. 403 (1877).
Mallory v. Pioneer Press, 26 N.W. 904 (Minn. 1884).
Marks v. Baker, 9 N.W. 678 (1881).
Matthew v. Beach, 7 N.Y. Sup. Ct. 256 (1851).
Metcalf v. Times Publishing Co., 40 A. 864 (R.I. 1898).
Miner v. Post Tribune, 49 Mich. 358 (1882).
Moore v. Stevenson, 27 Conn. 14 (1858).
Neeb v. Hope, 17 W.N.C. 93 (Pa. 1885).
Negley v. Farrow, 60 Md. 158 (1882).
Palmer v. City of Concord, 48 N.H. 211 (1868).
Park v. Detroit Free Press, 72 Mich. 560 (1888).
People v. Croswell, 3 Johns. Cas. 337 (N.Y. 1804).
People v. Few, 2 Johns. 290 (N.Y. 1807).
People v. Wilson, 64 Ill. 195 (1872).
Peoples v. Detroit Post & Tribune, 54 Mich. 457 (1885).
Pittock v. O'Neil, 63 Pa. 253 (1869).
Press Co. v. Stewart, 14 A. 51 (Pa. 1888).
Regensperger v. Kiefer, 7 A. 724, 725 (Pa. 1887).
Respublica v. Passmore, 3 Yeates 440 (Pa. 1802).
Riley v. Lee, 11 S.W. 713 (Ky. 1889).
Root v. King, 7 Cow. 613, 9 N.Y. Com. Law. Rpts. 609 (1827).
Sanford v. Bennett, 24 N.Y. 20 (1861).
Scripps v. Foster, 41 Mich. 742 (1879).
Scripps v. Reilly, 38 Mich. 10 (1878).

Sheckell v. Jackson, 64 Mass. 25 (1852).
Smith v. Tribune, 22 F. Cas. 689 (N.D. Ill. 1867) (No. 13,118).
Snyder v. Fulton, 34 Md. 128 (1870).
State v. Dunham, 6 Iowa 245 (1857).
State v. Frew and Hart, 24 W.Va. 416 (1884).
State v. Galloway, 5 Coldwell 326 (Tenn. 1868).
State v. Van Wye, 37 S.W. 938 (Mo. 1896).
Storey v. People, 79 Ill. 45 (1875).
Storey v. Wallace, 60 Ill. 51 (1871).
Strom v. People, 43 N.E. 622 (Ill. 1896).
Struthers & Sons v. The Evening Bulletin, 3 W.N.C. 215 (1877).
Stuart v. People, 4 Ill. (3 Scam.) 395 (1842).
Telegram Newspaper Co. v. Commonwealth, 52 N.E. 445 (Mass. 1899).
Thompson v. State, 17 Tex. Crim. 253 (1884).
Tresca v. Maddox, 11 La. Ann. 206 (1856).
United States v. Duane, 25 F. Cas. 920 (Pa. Crt. Ct. 1801).
United States v. Holmes, 26 F. Cas. 360 (E.D. Pa. 1842).
Upton v. Hume, 33 P. 810 (Oreg. 1893).
Usher v. Severance, 20 Maine 9 (1841).
Van Derverer v. Sutphin, 5 Ohio 293 (1855).
Wilson v. Fitch, 41 Calif. 363 (1871).

TWENTIETH-CENTURY APPELLATE COURT CASES

Abrams v. United States, 250 U.S. 616 (1919).
Coleman v. MacLennan, 98 P. 281 (Kan. 1908).
Curtis Publishing v. Butts, 388 U.S. 130 (1967).
Debs v. United States, 249 U.S. 211 (1919).
Dun & Bradstreet, Inc. v. Greenmoss Builders, Inc., 105 S. Ct. 2939 (1985).
First National Bank of Boston v. Bellotti, 435 U.S. 765 (1978).
Frohwerk v. United States, 249 U.S. 204 (1919).
Gertz v. Robert Welch, Inc., 418 U.S. 323 (1974).
Gitlow v. New York, 268 U.S. 325 (1925).
Griffin v. Kentucky Post, 10 M.L.R. (BNA) 605 (Ky. Crt. Ct. 1983).
Hepps v. Philadelphia Newspapers, 475 U.S. 767 (1986).
Houchins v. KQED, 438 U.S. 1 (1978).
Milkovich v. News-Herald, 473 N.E. 2d. 1191 (Ohio 1984).
Near v. Minnesota, 283 U.S. 697 (1931).

New York Times v. United States, 403 U.S. 713 (1971).
Ollman v. Evans, 750 F. 2d. 970 (C.A. D.C. 1984), *cert. denied*, 86 L. Ed. 2d. 278, 280 (1985).
Patterson v. Colorado, 205 U.S. 454 (1907).
Pell v. Procunier, 417 U.S. 817 (1974).
Richmond Newspapers v. Virginia, 448 U.S. 555 (1980).
Rosenblatt v. Baer, 383 U.S. 75 (1966).
Rosenbloom v. Metromedia, Inc., 403 U.S. 29 (1971).
Saxbe v. Washington Post, 417 U.S. 843 (1974).
Schenck v. United States, 249 U.S. 47 (1919).
Sheppard v. Maxwell, 384 U.S. 333 (1965).
Tavoulareas v. Washington Post, 759 F. 2d. 90 (C.A. D.C. 1985).
United States v. Carolene Products, 304 U.S. 144 (1938).
Westmoreland v. CBS, 10 M.L.R.(BNA) 2417 (S.D.N.Y. 1984).
Whitney v. California, 274 U.S. 357 (1927).

SELECTED BOOKS AND JOURNAL ARTICLES

Abraham, Henry J. *Freedom and the Court*. 4th ed. New York: Oxford Univ. Press, 1982.

Abrams, Floyd. "The Press is Different: Reflections on Justice Stewart and the Autonomous Press." *Hofstra Law Review* 7 (1979): 591.

————. "Why We Should Change the Libel Law." *New York Times Magazine*, 29 September 1985, 34.

Adler, Renata. *Reckless Disregard*. New York: Alfred A. Knopf, 1986.

Anderson, David A. "The Origins of the Press Clause." *UCLA Law Review* 30 (1983): 455.

————. "Reputation, Compensation, and Proof." *William and Mary Law Review* 25 (1984): 747.

Auerbach, Jerold S. *Unequal Justice*. New York: Oxford Univ. Press, 1976.

Bailyn, Bernard. *The Ideological Origins of the American Revolution*. Cambridge: Belknap Press of Harvard Univ., 1967.

Baldasty, Gerald J. "A Theory of Freedom of the Press: Massachusetts Newspapers and Law, 1782–1791." Master's thesis: Univ. of Wisconsin, Madison, 1974.

————. "The Press and Politics In the Age of Jackson." *Journalism Monographs* 89 (August 1984).

Bezanson, Randall P., Gilbert Cranberg, and John Soloski. "Libel Law and the Press: Setting the Record Straight." *Iowa Law Review* 71 (1985): 215.

Blanchard, Margaret A. "Filling the Void: Speech and Press in State Courts prior to *Gitlow*." In *The First Amendment Reconsidered*, edited by Bill F. Chamberlain and Charlene J. Brown. New York: Longman, 1982, 14.

Blasi, Vincent. "The Checking Value in First Amendment Theory." *American Bar Foundation Research Journal* 3 (1977): 541.

Botein, Stephen. "Printers and the American Revolution." In *The Press and the American Revolution*, edited by Bernard Bailyn and John B. Hench. Worcester: American Antiquarian Society, 1980.

Brown, Henry Billing. "The Liberty of the Press." *American Law Review* 34 (1900): 321.

Carter, Barton, Marc A. Franklin, and Jay B. Wright. *The First Amendment and the Fourth Estate*. Mineola, N.Y.: Foundation Press, 1985.

Chafee, Zechariah. *Free Speech in the United States*. 1920. Reprint. Cambridge: Harvard Univ. Press, 1942.

Chamberlain, William F. "Freedom of Expression in Eighteenth Century Connecticut." In *Newsletters to Newspapers*, edited by Donovan H. Bond and W. R. McLeod. Morgantown: School of Journalism, W. Va. Univ., 1977, 247–61.

Chase, George. "Criticism of Public Officers and Candidates for Office." *American Law Review* 23 (1889): 346.

Chauncey, Charles. "Contempt of Court." *American Law Register* 20 (1881): 220.

Cohen, Jeremy. *Congress Shall Make No Law: Oliver Wendell Holmes, the First Amendment, and Judicial Decision Making*, Ames: Iowa State Univ. Press, 1989.

Cooley, Thomas. *A Treatise on the Constitutional Limitations Which Rest upon the Legislative Power of the States of the American Union*, 2nd ed. Boston: Little, Brown & Co., 1871.

———. *Law of Torts*. Chicago: Callaghan & Co., 1879.

———, ed. *Blackstone Commentaries*. 4th ed., vol. 4. Chicago: Callahan & Co., 1899.

Cooper, Thomas. *A Treatise on the Law of Libel and the Liberty of the Press*. 1830. Reprint. New York: Da Capo Press, 1970.

Cox, Archibald. "Foreword: Freedom of Expression in the Burger Court." *Harvard Law Review* 94 (1980): 71.

"Critical Notice: A Treatise on the Law of Slander and Libel." *American Law Magazine* 2 (1844): 255.

Dworkin, Ronald. *Taking Rights Seriously*. Cambridge: Harvard Univ. Press, 1978.

———. *A Matter of Principle*. Cambridge: Harvard Univ. Press, 1985.

Eaton, Joel D. "The American Law of Defamation through *Gertz v. Robert Welch, Inc.* and beyond: An Analytical Primer." *Virginia Law Review* 61 (1975): 1362.

Emerson, Thomas. *The System of Freedom of Expression.* New York: Random House, 1970.

Fox, Sir John. *History of Contempt of Court.* Oxford: Clarendon Press, 1927, 21.

Franklin, Marc. A. "Winners and Losers and Why: A Study of Defamation Litigation." *American Bar Foundation Research Journal* (1980): 795,

_____. "Suing the Media for Libel: A Litigation Study." *American Bar Foundation Research Journal* (1981): 455.

_____. "Good Names and Bad Law: A Critique of Libel Law and a Proposal." *University of San Francisco Law Review* 18 (1983): 1.

Friedman, Lawrence M. *A History of American Law.* New York: Simon and Schuster, 1973.

Gawalt, Gerald W. "Sources of Anti-Lawyer Sentiment in Massachusetts, 1740–1840." *The American Journal of Legal History* 14 (1969): 283.

_____. "Massachusetts Legal Education in Transition, 1766–1840." *The American Journal of Legal History* 27 (1983): 27.

Gordon, Robert W. "Critical Legal Histories." *Stanford Law Review* 36 (1984): 57.

Grimke, Frederick. *The Nature and Tendency of Free Institutions,* edited by John William Ward. 1871. Reprint. Cambridge: Belknap Press of Harvard Univ., 1968.

Hallen, John E. "Fair Comment." *Texas Law Review* 8 (1929): 41.

Hamburger, Philip. "The Development of the Law of Seditious Libel and the Control of the Press." *Stanford Law Review* 37 (1985): 662.

Horwitz, Morton J. *The Transformation of American Law, 1780–1860.* Cambridge: Harvard Univ. Press, 1977.

_____. "Progressive Legal Historiography." *Oregon Law Review* 63 (1984): 679.

Hurst, James Willard. *The Growth of American Law.* Boston: Little, Brown & Co., 1950.

Jacobs, Clyde E. *Law Writers and the Courts.* Berkeley: Univ. of California Press, 1954.

Kalven, Harry, Jr. *The Negro and the First Amendment.* Columbus: Ohio State University, 1965.

Karst, Kenneth L. "Equality as a Central Principle in the First Amendment." *University of Chicago Law Review* 43 (1975): 20.

Lahav, Pnina, ed. *Press Law In Modern Democracies*. New York: Longman, 1985.

Lawhorne, Clifton O. *Defamation and Public Officials*. Carbondale: Southern Illinois Press, 1971.

Lee, Alfred McClung. *The Daily Newspaper in America*. New York: Macmillan Co., 1937.

Levy, Leonard W. *Emergence of a Free Press*. New York: Oxford Univ. Press, 1985.

———. "The *Legacy* Reexamined." *Stanford Law Review* 37 (1985): 769.

———, ed. *Freedom of the Press from Zenger to Jefferson*. Bobbs-Merrill Co., 1966.

Lewis, Anthony. "A Public Right to Know About Public Institutions: The First Amendment as a Sword." *Supreme Court Review* (1980): 19.

———. *New York Times v. Sullivan* Reconsidered: Time to Return to 'The Central Meaning of the First Amendment.' " *Columbia Law Review* 83 (1983): 603.

——— "Annals of Law: The Sullivan Case." *New Yorker,* 5 November 1984, 52.

Madison, James. *The Virginia Report of 1799–1800*. 1800. Reprint. New York: Da Capo Press, 1970.

Malone, Dumas. *The Public Life of Thomas Cooper*. New Haven: Yale Univ. Press, 1926.

Meiklejohn, Alexander. *Political Freedom*. New York: Oxford Univ. Press, 1948.

Merrill, Samuel. *Newspaper Libel*. Boston: Ticknor & Co., 1888.

Mill, John S. *On Liberty in Utilitarianism, on Liberty, and Considerations on Representative Government*. 1859. Reprint, edited by H. B. Acton. New York: E. P. Dutton, 1976.

Miller, Charles. *The Supreme Court and the Uses of History*. Cambridge: Belknap Press of Harvard Univ., 1969.

Miller, John E. *The Federalist Era*. New York: Harper & Row, 1960.

Miller, Perry. *The Life of the Mind in America*. New York: Harcourt Brace and World, 1965.

Milton, John. *Areopagitica*. 1644. Reprint. Edited with an introduction by Sir Richard C. Jebb. Oxford: Oxford Univ. Press, 1940.

Murphy, Paul. "Time to Reclaim: The Current Challenge of American Constitutional History." *American Historical Review* 69 (1963): 77.

Nagel, Robert F. "How to Stop Libel Suits and Still Protect Individual Reputation." *Washington Monthly* (November 1985): 12.

Nelles, Walter and Carol Weiss King. "Contempt by Publication in the United States: To the Federal Contempt Statute." *Columbia Law Review* 28 (1928): 401.

Nelson, Harold L. *Libel in News of Congressional Investigating Committees.* Minneapolis: Univ. of Minnesota Press, 1961.

Paterson, James. *The Liberty of the Press, Speech, and Public Worship.* London: Macmillian Co., 1880.

Pember, Don R. "Founders (Meeting in Secret) Protected Our Right to Publish, But Not to Gather the News." *Bulletin of the American Society of Newspaper Editors* (Dec./Jan. 1979).

_____. *Mass Media Law.* 3d. ed. Dubuque: Wm. C. Brown, 1984.

Perry, Michael J. "Freedom of Expression: An Essay on Theory and Doctrine." *Northwestern University Law Review* 78 (1984): 1197.

Rapalje, Stewart. *A Treatise on Contempt.* New York: L. K. Strouse & Co., 1890.

Redish, Martin H. "The Value of Free Speech." *University of Pennsylvania Law Review* 130 (1982): 591.

Rosenberg, Norman L. "Thomas M. Cooley, Liberal Jurisprudence, and the Law of Libel, 1868–1884." *University of Puget Sound Law Review* 4 (1980): 49.

_____. *Protecting the Best Men.* Chapel Hill: Univ. of North Carolina Press, 1985.

Sack, Robert B. "Reflections on the Wrong Question: Special Constitutional Privilege for the Institutional Press." *Hofstra Law Review* 7 (1979): 629.

Scanlon, Thomas. "A Theory of Freedom of Expression." *Philosophy and Public Affairs* 1 (1972): 204.

Schiffler, Kenneth. "Fifty-one First Amendments: State Constitutions and Freedom of Expression." Master's thesis, Univ. of Washington, 1985.

Schiller, Dan. *Objectivity and the News.* Philadelphia: Univ. of Pennsylvania Press, 1981.

Schudson, Michael. *Discovering the News.* New York: Basic Books, 1978.

Siebert, Frederick S. *Freedom of the Press in England, 1476–1776.* 1952. Reprint. Urbana: Univ. of Illinois Press, 1965.

Smith, James Morton. *Freedom's Fetters.* Ithaca: Cornell Univ. Press, 1956.

Smith, Jeffery A. *Printer and Press Freedom.* New York: Oxford Univ. Press, 1988.

Smolla, Rodney A. "Let the Author Beware: The Rejuvenation of the American Law of Libel." *University of Pennsylvania Law Review* 132 (1983): 1.

_____. *Suing the Press.* New York: Oxford Univ. Press, 1986.

Sowle, Kathryn Dix. "Defamation and the First Amendment." *New York University Law Review* 54 (1979): 478.

Starkie, Thomas. *A Treatise on the Law of Slander, Libel and Scandalum Magnatum.* New York: Collins & Harmany, 1832.

Stevens, John. "Criminal Libel as Seditious Libel, 1916–65." *Journalism Quarterly* 43 (1966): 110.

Stewart, Potter. "Or of the Press." *Hastings Law Review* 26 (1975): 633.

Story, Joseph. *Commentaries on the Constitution of the United States.* Boston: Little, Brown & Co., 1833.

_____. *A Familiar Exposition of the Constitution of the United States.* New York: Harper and Bros., 1852.

Teeter, Dwight L., Jr. "King Sears, the Mob and Freedom of the Press in New York, 1765–76." *Journalism Quarterly* 41 (1964): 539.

_____. "The Printer and the Chief Justice: Seditious Libel in 1782–83." *Journalism Quarterly* 45 (1968): 445.

Thomas, Cromwell H. *Problems of Contempt of Court.* Baltimore: Author, 1934.

Tiedeman, Christopher. *A Treatise on the Limitations of Police Power in the United States.* St. Louis: F. H. Thomas Law Book Co., 1886.

Townshend, John. *A Treatise on the Wrongs Called Slander and Libel.* 4th. ed. sec. 209. New York: Baker Voorhis & Co., 1890.

Tribe, Laurence H. *Constitutional Choices.* Cambridge: Harvard Univ. Press, 1985.

Tucker, St. George, ed. *Blackstone Commentaries.* Philadelphia: William Young Birch and Abraham Small [Shaw-Shoemaker Early Am. Imp.], 1803.

Van Alstyne, William W. "First Amendment Limitations on Recovery from the Press — An Extended Comment on the 'Anderson Solution.' " *William and Mary Law Review* 24 (1984): 793.

_____. *Interpretations of the First Amendment.* Durham: Duke Univ. Press Policy Studies, 1984.

Veeder, Van Vechten. "History and Theory of Law of Defamation." *Columbia Law Review* 3 (1903): 546.

Walsh, Justin E. *To Print the News and Raise Hell.* Chapel Hill: Univ. of North Carolina Press, 1968.

White, Edward. *The American Judicial Tradition.* New York: Oxford Univ. Press, 1976.

Wortman, Tunis. *A Treatise Concerning Political Inquiry and the Liberty of the Press.* 1800. Reprint. New York: Da Capo Press, 1970.

INDEX

Abrams, Floyd
and the institutional press, 5
and libel law, 106
American Newspaper Publishers
Association, 66, 101, 113
Anderson, David, 11
Arnold v. Clifford, 63
Arnold v. Saying Co., 76–77n
Atkinson v. Detroit Press, 71n

Bailey v. Kalamazoo Publishing,
69n, 72n
Bailyn, Bernard, 17
and opposition ideology, 24–27
Barnes v. Campbell, 75n
*Bathrick v. Detroit Post & Tribune
Co.,* 72n
Bennett, James Gordon, 64
Black, Hugo, 6
Blackstone's Commentaries. See also
Thomas Cooley; Joseph Story;
St. George Tucker
William Blackstone and freedom
of the press, 3
Blasi, Vincent
and checking value theory, 59
and the institutional press, 5
Boies, David, Jr., 109
Botein, Stephen, 11
*Bourreseau v. Detroit Evening
Journal Co.,* 70
Brandeis, Louis, 3
Brennan, William, 104, 105
Brown, Henry B., 49
Buel, Richard, 25
Byers v. Martin, 68n

Cato (John Trenchard and Thomas
Gordon), 24–26
Chafee, Jr., Zechariah, 37–38
Cheadle v. State, 95–96n
Chicago (Ill.) *Daily American,* 85, 88
Chicago (Ill.) *Evening Journal,* 92
Chicago (Ill.) *Times,* 68, 93
Clark, Tom, 6
Coleman v. MacLennan, 57–58
Common law
definition of, 41
priveleges in, 54–57
Commonwealth v. Clap, 58n
Commonwealth v. David Lee Child,
53n
Commonwealth v. Wright, 64n
Content by publication
definition of, 83–85
Federal Contempt Statue of 1831,
86
Cooley, Thomas
and common-law privileges, 56–
57, 71, 72
Constitutional Limitations, 47–48
influence on freedom of the press,
47
and legal treatises, 45
and meaning of freedom of the
press, 39, 48
on watchdog duty, 70
Cooper, Thomas, 34
Cooper v. People ex rel. Wyatt, 94–
95n
Cox, Archibald, 6
Curry v. Walter, 57

Daily Chronotype, 64